Dinosaur
Dictionary
for Kids

The Everything Guide for
Kids Who Love Dinosaurs

Dinosaur
Dictionary
for Kids

Bob Korpella

PRUFROCK PRESS INC.
WACO, TEXAS

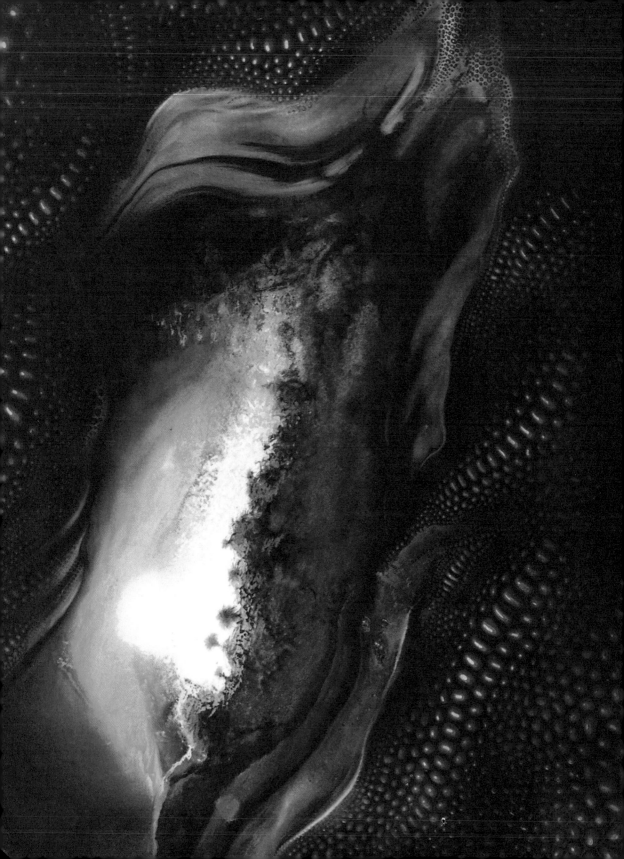

Dedication

For Brooklyn Horner and Kierce Horner

Library of Congress Cataloging-in-Publication Data

Names: Korpella, Bob, author.
Title: Dinosaur dictionary for kids : the everything guide for kids who love
  dinosaurs / by Bob Korpella.
Description: Waco, Texas : Prufrock Press Inc., [2016] | Audience: Grades 4
  to 6. | Includes bibliographical references and index.
Identifiers: LCCN 2016010050 | ISBN 9781618215130 (pbk.)
Subjects: LCSH: Dinosaurs--Juvenile literature. | Dinosaurs--Dictionaries,
  Juvenile.
Classification: LCC QE861.3 .K67 2016 | DDC 567.903--dc23
LC record available at http://lccn.loc.gov/2016010050

Edited by Katy McDowall

Cover and layout design by Raquel Trevino

ISBN-13: 978-1-61821-513-0

Printed in the United States of America.

At the time of this book's publication, all facts and figures cited are the most current available. All telephone numbers, addresses, and website URLs are accurate and active. All publications, organizations, websites, and other resources exist as described in the book, and all have been verified. The author and Prufrock Press Inc. make no warranty or guarantee concerning the information and materials given out by organizations or content found at websites, and we are not responsible for any changes that occur after this book's publication. If you find an error, please contact Prufrock Press Inc.

Prufrock Press Inc.
P.O. Box 8813
Waco, TX 76714-8813
Phone: (800) 998-2208
Fax: (800) 240-0333
http://www.prufrock.com

Table of Contents

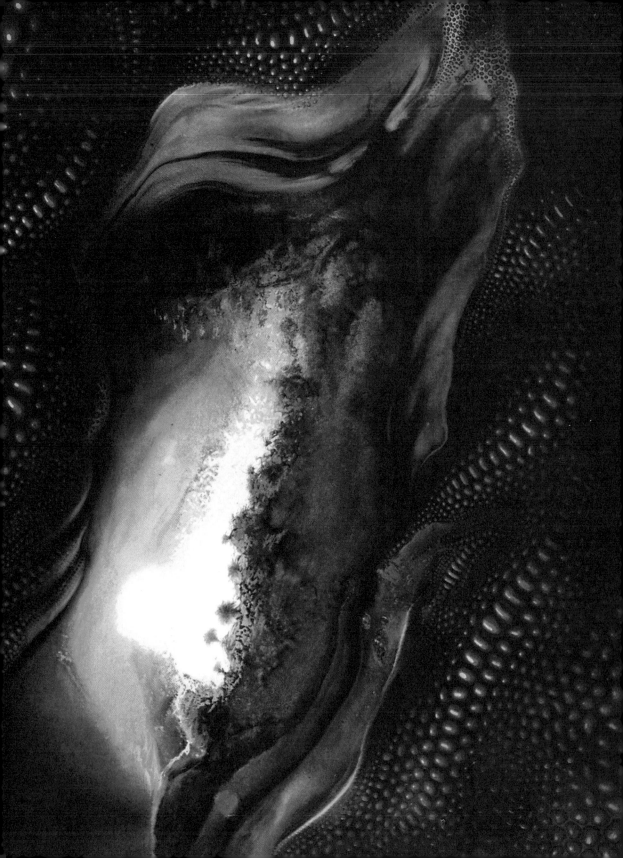

Acknowledgements

As a naturalist, I'm excited to learn and discover the natural history of life in our world. For me, that usually means aquatic insects and invertebrates, mammals, fish, dragonflies, and damselflies. But dinosaurs present a most incredible journey far back in time to a place we can only begin to imagine. For me, that journey has been enlightening and delightful. I am thankful for all those who shared a portion of the voyage with me:

Helyn, who has always kept me centered and on track, and for her belief in me as I remade my profession, and for her undying support in that quest. Her smile brightens my day and makes me certain I can tackle any task that lies ahead.

Mom, for her constant encouragement and belief that I can make a success of any project I take on. And for the memory of my Dad, always with me in spirit.

Elizabeth, Megan, Brooklyn, and Kierce for their eternal excitement in this project.

The Springfield Chapter of Missouri Master Naturalists, who demonstrated their support in this endeavor from the onset. That support never wavered. This is a most incredible group of people, the finest of which I have ever had the pleasure of being a part.

Hunter, because he is a bright young student with a bold future. His enthusiasm and knowledge of dinosaurs and their world was an inspiration.

Mary Anning and all the early paleontologists whose discoveries brought to light an amazing era in the Earth's history. Their research and discoveries launched a movement that survives to this day.

Curious children everywhere whose fascination keeps dinosaurs alive for all of us.

All the folks at Prufrock Press for the design, layout, and production of this book. A very special thanks to Katy McDowall, for the excellent direction she provided, for editing this book, and for her patience with me throughout the process, and Raquel Trevino for her outstanding design from cover to cover, as well as the many illustrators who contributed their art.

This remarkable trip means I will never look at the world in quite the same way again. The realization that incredible beasts roamed the same places where I've lived, or that swimming reptiles and ancient fish populated the shallow sea close to where I make my home today give new perspective to the past. Researching and writing this book erased the eons of time between the age of dinosaurs and us, breathing new life into how I imagine the planet looked and behaved long ago. My sincere hope is that you, too, will find the same awe and wonder that I did as you take your own journey back in time while reading this book.

Argentinosaurus

Introduction to the Mesozoic Era

Picturing dinosaurs and the world in which they lived tickles the imagination. Creatures that disappeared from the planet 65 million years ago become vivid in our minds as we read and study them. But think about it—some of the biggest animals to have ever roamed the Earth may have walked across what is now your back yard. Their fossilized bones may rest beneath your own basement!

Spinosaurus and Psittacosaurus

Paleontologists constantly find new information about the Mesozoic Era—the time of the dinosaurs—through new discoveries, research on bones stored away and forgotten, or new experiments that reveal details that scientists centuries ago could not have dreamed.

What color were dinosaurs? That is becoming clearer than ever before. Are birds really related to those gigantic beasts of the past? The links are surprising and the evidence mounting. Did dinosaurs communicate with sounds? Some, it appears, did exactly that. Were any dinosaurs feathered? Yes—more than you might realize.

Not every discovery comes from a trained paleontologist. A 14-year-old boy made one new discovery—a dinosaur named Bambiraptor after the famous Disney character. Mary Anning walked the beaches of England in the 1800s, searching for fossils she documented with incredible accuracy. Fossils sometimes show up in farmers' fields, when workers build a bridge, or when rocks are dug from a quarry. Touching a fossil, seeing one on display in a museum, or reading about the dinosaur that left the remains brings it all a little closer to home.

After all, dinosaurs perished about 65 million years ago after surviving through incredible changes in the world for 186 million years. That length of time proves difficult to visualize. Imagine a piece of paper representing one year. Stack 10 or 15 papers and they represent a student who is 10 or 15 years old. It's not a very tall stack. A ream of computer paper is around 2 inches high and contains 500 sheets of paper, or 500 years. Piling reams of paper to represent 65 million years would result in a stack about 20,000 feet high, the cruising altitude of a small jet. And that represents how long ago the last dinosaur vanished. The stack of papers reaching back to when dinosaurs first appeared would be about 80,000 feet high, or about 15 miles.

The world then was much different than the world in which we live today. The time period from about 250 million years ago to 65 million years ago is called the Mesozoic Era. That time frame is further divided into three periods: the Triassic, the Jurassic, and the Cretaceous. Dinosaurs in one form or another lived during all three of those times.

Brachiosaurus

As the world changed, so did the dinosaurs. Most started out modestly sized. They usually moved on two hind legs. Some were predators; others ate tough plant material. As time passed, dinosaurs evolved into larger and much larger giants. Leaves and vegetation were plentiful and dinosaurs consumed a lot of them. Predators had to evolve, too, or they would never have been able to attack and kill the mighty beasts for food. As more time passed, the hides of prey toughened and some even grew armor. Predator's teeth had to grow longer and their jaws needed to become more powerful.

Albertaceratops

Even though dinosaurs were the dominant species during the Mesozoic Era, they were not the only animals on the planet. Reptiles were everywhere, scurrying among leaf litter on forest floors, flying through the skies, and swimming in the waters. Insects such as spiders, dragonflies, and cockroaches also lived during the era. Mammals were just beginning to get their start in the world. They would not rise to domination until the next era.

By the time the Mesozoic Era wound to a close, dinosaurs had become incredibly diverse and different. Other animal life on Earth was starting to compete with them for space and food, but dinosaurs continued to adapt to a changing world the same as they had done for millions of years. Then everything crashed. A great extinction took more than 70% of all life on the planet, including the large dinosaurs. Scientists still debate the cause of the extinction, but that picture is also becoming clearer.

Hopefully, this book will fuel your desire to understand more about dinosaurs and the time in which they lived. Even if you have just a passing thought or two about these mighty animals, you may find new information that fans the flames of learning inside you. Maybe you will look differently at the birds stopping by your feeders, or want to explore a natural history museum, perhaps visit a place like Dinosaur National Park. It's an exciting world. Learn all you can of it.

Note on Using the Dictionary

This book has three sections devoted to describing some of the dinosaurs discovered over the past several centuries. Those sections are divided into the three periods of the Mesozoic Era—the Triassic, the Jurassic, and the Cretaceous—and each has an alphabetical listing of the dinosaurs that lived during those time periods. Each dinosaur's entry lists:

◈ its genus name;

◈ how to pronounce the name;

◈ how long ago it lived (mya, or million years ago);

◈ its estimated length in feet;

◈ its estimated weight in pounds;

◈ the country, state, or region where its fossils were discovered;

◈ its diet (carnivore, herbivore, omnivore); and

◈ a description and facts about the dinosaur.

You'll also discover other animals of the Mesozoic Era, including reptiles, insects, and mammals, as well as fascinating sidebars about experiments, important people, and other dinosaur facts. Digging Deeper sections will take you on in-depth explorations of several important topics, including the link between dinosaurs and birds and—of course—extinction. The Dinosaur Bites section provides activities and other resources, including a quiz and tips for fossil hunting. If you find a few words that you do not understand, the following section on basic terms of the Mesozoic Era may help you.

Spinosaurus

Basic Terms of the Mesozoic Era

Abelisaur: A carnivorous dinosaur family characterized by walking on two powerful legs, and having small arms and skulls that are nearly equal in height and length.

Ankylosaur: Armor-plated dinosaurs with short legs.

Bipedal: An animal that uses two legs to walk.

Carnivore: An animal that eats the flesh of other animals.

Cretaceous: The third and final time period of the Mesozoic Era. It began around 145 million years ago and lasted until about 65 million years ago.

Diurnal: Active during daylight hours.

Frill: A large projection of bone around the neck of a dinosaur. Some were round, others elongated. Typically included several horns.

Gastrolith: Stones swallowed to aid in digesting plant matter.

Genus: A group of animals that share similar characteristics. A genus fits within the larger grouping of *family*. Below genus is *species*. The genus name is always capitalized.

Herbivore: A plant-eating animal.

Insectivore: An insect-eating animal.

Jurassic: The second time period of the Mesozoic Era. It lasted from the end of the Triassic Period around 201 million years ago until the start of the Cretaceous Period 145 million years ago.

Mesozoic: A span of time defined by changes in the geology of the Earth. Sometimes called the "Age of the Dinosaur," it lasted from about 250 million years ago to about 65 million years ago.

mya: An abbreviation for "million years ago."

Naris: Another word for nostril. *Nares* is plural.

Nocturnal: Active during nighttime hours.

Omnivore: An animal that eats both plants and the flesh of other animals.

Ornithischian: One of the two main dinosaur orders. These animals had hip-bones that faced toward the rear, just like those of modern birds. In fact, the name means "bird-hipped." All ornithischians were herbivores as the hipbone placement left more room for the digestive organs needed to break down tough plant material. Despite the name, modern birds did not evolve from this order.

Ornithopod: A plant-eating dinosaur that walked on two legs.

Paleontologist: A scientist who studies past geological eras using the fossils left behind from those time periods.

Piscivorous: Consuming a diet of fish.

Prosauropod: A less formal name for the plant-eating sauropodomorphs that walked on two legs and evolved into the huge herbivores that walked on all fours.

Quadruped: A dinosaur that walked on all fours.

Saurischian: One of the two main orders of dinosaurs. The name means "lizard-hipped" and it refers to the hipbone, which faced forward or down in these dinosaurs. All meat-eating dinosaurs were saurischian. A few, such as Diplodocus, were herbivores. Modern birds evolved from saurischians rather than the bird-hipped ornithischians.

Sauropod: Gigantic plant-eating beasts with long necks, long tails, and pillar-like legs.

Sauropodomorph: A category of dinosaurs that were herbivores with long necks. The earliest forms were small and walked on two legs. Sauropodomorphs eventually developed into the massive plant eaters such as Diplodocus.

Scute: A thick, bony plate or a large scale on the back of an armored dinosaur.

Species: A group within a genus with individuals sharing some common features among them.

Stegosaur: A plant-eating dinosaur with a small head that walked on all fours. These dinosaurs had a double row of plates or spikes along their backs.

Theropod: A group of saurischian dinosaurs with teeth that were serrated like the edge of a steak knife. They all walked on hind legs only, and their bone structure included a wishbone, like those in modern birds. Most theropods were carnivores, but a few evolved into plant eaters.

TAXONOMY

Taxonomy is the name for the process of how scientists classify organisms. A taxonomic rank is a list of how these organisms are divided into categories. The categories get defined more narrowly with each step until we know the exact species of the organism. Taxonomy helps show how different organisms relate to one another. The major categories include:

→ **Kingdom:** Dinosaurs belong to Animalia, or animal kingdom, the same as us.
→ **Phylum:** Dinosaurs and people also belong to the same phylum, Chordata.
→ **Class:** Dinosaurs are considered Archosauria, while people are Mammalia, or mammals.
→ **Order:** Dinosaurs belong to one of two orders, depending on the shape of their hipbones. Ornithischians had bird-shaped hips and Saurischians had lizard-shaped hips.
→ **Family:** There are a lot of dinosaur families, each with distinct characteristics (bone structure, feeding habits, movements, etc.).
→ **Genus:** Families share characteristics, but genus sets dinosaurs in the same family apart (maybe the shape of their teeth, the power of their jaws, or size differs). Genus is the dinosaur name with which we are most familiar (Tyrannosaurus, Velociraptor, Stegosaurus, etc.).
→ **Species:** Very subtle differences separate species within a genus. We do not often include a dinosaur species when we talk about individuals (however, a notable exception is Tyrannosaurus rex, where *rex* is the species).

Triassic: The first and earliest time period in the Mesozoic Era. It stretched from about 250 million years ago to the start of the Jurassic Period about 201 million years ago.

Troodon: An individual dinosaur belonging to a family that was fairly small, with long legs and huge brains compared to other dinosaurs. These dinosaurs also had a curved claw on the second toe. They had excellent hearing and forward-facing eyes.

Tyrannosaur: The most well known of the carnivores. They walked on two legs and had large, powerful jaws and small arms.

Vertebra: Each individual bone making up the backbone of an animal.

Sauropod Heart Health

A perplexing question facing paleontologists is how the giant sauropods pumped blood all the way up to their heads, seemingly in defiance of gravity. Scientists estimate that the heart of a Barosaurus would have to weigh several tons in order to have enough strength to pump blood up its nearly 50-foot neck. Columbia University researchers calculated that the blood pressure required to make that happen would have to be 700 mm of mercury or more. By comparison, a person's blood pressure is only about 120 mm of mercury. That high a pressure could damage the small blood vessels inside a Barosaurus's lungs. Plus, the Columbia researchers reckoned that a heart as massive as scientists estimate would pump blood so slowly that it would all pour back down the neck before the next heartbeat.

How do you think these giant beasts were able to get blood all the way up their necks to their heads? Give it some thought before finding what paleontologists think on page 10.

6 FEET

Apatosaurus

DIGGING DEEPER

How Do We Know What We Know About Dinosaurs?

No human has ever seen a dinosaur. People did not appear on the planet until about 64 million years after the last dinosaur was gone. So how can paleontologists determine what a dinosaur looked like, what it ate, how it moved, and even tell one dinosaur from another?

The process begins when dinosaur fossils first emerge from the ground. They are often encased in rock and covered by layers of sand and dirt. This has to be carefully removed in order to preserve the fine details as much as possible. It may take months or even years to extract the bones, especially if they belong to a complete or nearly complete skeleton.

Once the bones are free of the ground, they must be cataloged, packaged, and shipped to a museum or laboratory for further study. Paleontologists take precise measurements as they examine every bit of each bone or bone fragment. They write down everything they observe.

Close attention to all of the details in fossilized bones helps scientists decide whether a bone belongs to a known dinosaur, a different species of a known dinosaur, or a whole new discovery. The shapes of the bones, how the joints are designed, where tendons attached, and the size of the bones are all clues in identifying the discovery.

Sometimes scientists get lucky and find a dinosaur with mummified remains. That means the skin, soft tissues like internal organs, and sometimes even the food a dinosaur ate have been preserved for millions of years. The perfect set of conditions must exist underground before mummification occurs. Most often, the soft tissues melt away and only the hard bones turn into fossils. When paleontologists find a mummified remains, they get much more information about diets, how muscles attached, the size of the organs, and more.

Clearly, mummified remains give scientists a more accurate picture of what the dinosaur was like. The rest of the time, researchers must compare all of the information they have on a new find to what they already know about other dinosaur discoveries.

For example, measuring how tall a leg bone is and how large it is around gives a good idea of how much the dinosaur weighed when it was alive. That same bone might also hint at how fast or slow the dinosaur moved, and from that information, whether it chased its prey as a theropod or plodded along like the huge sauropods.

Skulls in good condition are an especially good discovery, particularly if the teeth are still present. The shape of those teeth can tell scientists what the dinosaur ate. Hollow bones or solid, massive skull bones can indicate the dinosaur's behavior. The shape of the jaw might tell researchers how powerful the animal's bite was.

None of this process is quick. It can take many years to study all of the details presented by a new dinosaur find. Paleontologists want to make certain their information and assumptions about a dinosaur are as accurate as possible. They typically publish a paper on the find that is read by other paleontologists who might agree or disagree with the conclusions. If other paleontologists disagree with the findings, they might argue why in a paper of their own.

This process of debating what the gathered information means is part of how science creates the most accurate idea it can about an amazing and terrifying animal—some of the largest the world has ever known—that we will not meet face to face.

Sauropod Heart Health, Part II

Some paleontologists suggest that Barosaurus, and other large sauropods, had more than one heart. They wonder if these massive dinosaurs had several hearts that acted like relay stations all the way up the neck. Because internal organs and muscles do not fossilize well, the exact method dinosaurs used in circulating blood can only be theorized.

Another possibility is that large sauropods may have relied on a sort of valve system in their arteries that would squeeze blood rapidly up the neck between heartbeats.

A third theory is that sauropods did not use their long necks to reach the leaves and plant material at treetop level. Instead, they held their necks nearly horizontal to the ground. To eat, they swept their necks back and forth over lower growing vegetation, like a vacuum cleaner.

Did you guess any or all of these possibilities? Which do you think is most likely? Did you think of another possibility?

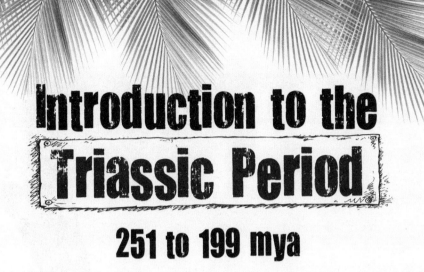

Introduction to the Triassic Period

251 to 199 mya

The world in Triassic times would not at all resemble the world in which we all live today. Polar ice caps were missing, and all of the continents were connected as one big land mass known as Pangaea. The interior of that land mass was nothing more than a hot, dry desert because the mass was so large that rain could not reach that far inland before evaporating. The coastal edges of Pangaea were green, as were river valleys. Days were a little shorter—about 22¾ hours long instead of 24—because the Earth rotated faster.

Triassic plants, many species of which still exist today, had tough leaves. Cycads, a palm-like tree, ginkgo, horsetails, and conifer trees all flourished in the temperate climate zones.

But the beginning of the Triassic Period and the end of the previous, the Permian Period, was marked by the largest mass extinction to have ever hit the Earth. It destroyed about 90% of life on the planet. Almost all trees were wiped out. Less than 5% of marine life survived, and less than one third of all large land animals made it. The exact cause of the extinction is not known, but it took millions of years for life to recover. Among the new species that found success in the Triassic world were dinosaurs.

Reptiles also found success in the new world. Some, the pterosaurs, took to the skies while others, such as Elasmosaurus, roamed the oceans. Mammals began to make an appearance as they evolved from reptile cousins.

Yet another mass extinction marked the end of the Triassic Period, but this one actually helped dinosaurs. They were left unaffected while many of their competitors for food and territory vanished.

Blikanasaurus (bli-KAHN-oh-SORE-us)

Age: 216–203 mya
Size: 16 ft long
Weight: 550 lbs
Location: Lesotho
Food: Herbivore

Blikanasaurus is the earliest known example of a dinosaur that walked, ate, and spent the majority of its time on all fours. Scientists determined this from a huge hind leg that, with its stout foot, looked like it could have belonged to a sauropod. Measurements of that leg section suggest a massively built dinosaur. The fossil came from Mount Blikana, which is where this dino got its name.

Chindesaurus (CHIN-dee-SORE-us)

Age: 227–210 mya
Size: 8 ft long
Weight: 33 lbs
Location: USA: Arizona, Texas, New Mexico
Food: Carnivore

A light and fast moving predator, the first fossils of this dinosaur were discovered in Arizona's Petrified Forest. Since then, scientists uncovered several partial specimens. They also found a single tooth from Chindesaurus, and it showed the serrated edges of a hunter. Chindesaurus had long legs and a tapered tail. Its name means "Chinde lizard" after the area where it was found.

Dracoraptor, from the Jurassic Period

Chromogisaurus (crow-moe-gi-SORE-us)

Age: 231 mya
Size: 7 ft long
Weight: 20 lbs
Location: Argentina
Food: Possibly an omnivore

A very primitive prosauropod that was just beginning to develop some of the features shared by sauropods. A Chromogisaurus skull has yet to be found, so scientists can only speculate on Chromogisaurus's diet. The name means "colored earth dinosaur," and it refers to the Painted Valley area of Argentina where the fossils emerged. American paleontologist Martin Daniel Ezcurra named the dinosaur in 2010.

Coelophysis (SEE-low-FYE-sis)

Age: 200 mya
Size: 10 ft long
Weight: 55 lbs
Location: USA: Arizona, New Mexico
Food: Carnivore

Coelophysis's name means "hollow form," and it describes its light, hollow bones. This meat eater had a long, narrow jaw edged in sharp teeth. Its slim body and long legs made it a fast moving predator. Large eye sockets indicate very keen eyesight. Walking on its hind legs, Coelophysis used its forearms for grasping its prey. It also had a wishbone, as do modern birds.

Coelophysis's fossilized bones were discovered in the Petrified Forest in Arizona. Paleontologist Edwin H. Colbert described finding hundreds more skeletons at Ghost Ranch, NM. Its remains flew into space aboard the space shuttle Endeavor, marking the second time a dinosaur visited space (Maiasaura was the first).

A small skeleton inside the stomach cavity of one Coelophysis was at first identified as a young specimen of the same species. Scientists speculated that Coelophysis ate the young or weak of its own kind. Later analysis showed that the skeleton belonged to a small, crocodile-like animal.

Daemonosaurus (DEE-mon-oh-SORE-us)

Age: 205 mya
Size: 5 ft long
Weight: 33 lbs
Location: USA: New Mexico
Food: Carnivore

Daemonosaurus was nicknamed the "buck-toothed dinosaur" because its upper teeth protrude forward. The species name, D. chauliodus, means buck-toothed. Daemonosaurus means "demon lizard," which refers to Ghost Ranch, NM, where legends say evil spirits inhabit the area. Daemonosaurus's teeth were sharp and its jaw lined with them. A lean, long-legged frame suggests that Daemonosaurus could move quickly. Its powerful jaws made it capable of penetrating deep into its prey.

Efraasia (eff-RAHS-ee-ah)

Age: 210 mya
Size: 20 ft long
Weight: 1,980 lbs
Location: Germany
Food: Herbivore

Eberhard Fraas found the remains of this dinosaur in 1909, and it was named in his honor in 1973. The skeleton proved to be that of a juvenile of the species. Efraasia probably walked on all fours. It could likely rear up on its hind legs in order to reach higher branches, grasping them with its long fingers. Its neck was beginning to get longer, but not nearly as long as those of its huge sauropod descendants. Most of what is known comes from a partial skull and a few other bones.

Eodromaeus (EE-oh-DROME-ee-us)

Age: 231 mya
Size: 4 ft long
Weight: 11 lbs
Location: Argentina
Food: Carnivore

The discovery of Eodromaeus in 2011 made paleontologists reconsider another early dinosaur, Eoraptor. Given a name that means "dawn runner," Eodromaeus was one of the earliest known dinosaurs in a family that would someday include Allosaurus and Tyrannosaurus. Eoraptor had once been given that title.

Eodromaeus was long and lean, with definite theropod features, such as serrated, knife-like teeth and grasping hands with long fingers. Its legs were long and built for speed. Some scientists estimate it may have traveled as fast as 19 mph.

Eoraptor (EE-oh-rap-tore)

Age: 230–225 mya
Size: 3 ft long
Weight: 22 lbs
Location: Argentina
Food: Possibly omnivore

Its name means "dawn thief" because it lived at the dawn of the age of dinosaurs. Ricardo Martinez found this fossil in 1991while working on a team headed by paleontologists Paul Sereno and Alfretto Monetta. They thought he had discovered the earliest known meat-eating dinosaur. In 2011, Sereno found an even earlier dinosaur, Eodromaeus, which had features more common in theropods. As a result, Sereno moved Eoraptor from the theropod tree to the sauropod tree.

The shape of Eoraptors's teeth made them well suited to eating both plant material and animals. Its hands and feet had sharp claws, and was most likely very fast. Its hips were lizard-like, and its body may have been covered in scales or feathers.

Herrerasaurus (her-AIR-ah-SORE-us)

Age: 231 mya
Size: 20 ft long
Weight: 772 lbs
Location: Argentina: San Juan
Food: Carnivore

Herrerasaurus was named for Victorino Herrera, who found the fossilized bones while herding goats in Argentina in 1959. An almost complete skeleton was found in 1988. Herrerasaurus's light bone structure made it a fast and stealthy predator. Its snout was long, its jaws lined with curved and pointed teeth. Herrerasaurus's jaw was hinged like those of some modern lizards. The double hinge allowed its mouth to open wider so it could grip its victim.

Isanosaurus (ee-sahn-oh-SORE-us)

Age: 216–199 mya
Size: 40 ft long
Weight: 2 tons
Location: Thailand
Food: Herbivore

A few vertebrae, some ribs and one 2-foot-long piece of thigh bone are all that were found of Isanosaurus. That was still enough for paleontologists to piece together some comparisons with related dinosaurs. They think that Isanosaurus walked on all fours with the ability to rear back on its hind legs for reaching. It probably had a very small head in comparison to the body. This dinosaur's bones were found in the Isan region of Thailand, from which Isanosaurus got its name.

Lesothosaurus (less-oh-tho-SORE-us)

Age: 200 mya
Size: 3 ft
Weight: 8 lbs
Location: Lesotho
Food: Herbivore

The "Lesotho lizard" was found in the Lesotho area of Africa and named by Peter Galton in 1978. It appeared just as the Triassic Period ended, and it died out by the middle of the Jurassic Period. It had the long hind legs and long toes of a quick runner. Lesothosaurus's teeth were set inward and it likely fed on low-growing vegetation. It had a stiffened tail for better balance and may have had a cheek pouch for storing and chewing food. Scientists think that Lesothosaurus may have moved in herds, scattering and running if danger arose.

Lessemsaurus (less-em-SORE-us)

Age: 210 mya
Size: 30 ft long
Weight: 1.7 tons
Location: Argentina
Food: Herbivore

A section of backbone is all that exists of this dinosaur, but that was enough to indicate that Lessemsaurus had spines along its back that formed a ridge. Scientists are not sure the purpose of the ridge. José Bonaparte named Lessemsaurus for Don Lessem, a science author nicknamed "Dino Dan." Many of Lessem's books discussed dinosaurs.

Liliensternus (lil-ee-en-STERN-us)

Age: 205 mya
Size: 17 ft long
Weight: 220 lbs
Location: Germany
Food: Carnivore

One of the largest and most formidable meat eaters of its time, its neck was long and slender, and its tail was equally long.

Liliensternus's head bore a long crest, which may have been covered with colorful skin for display. This dinosaur was named for Rühle von Lilienstern, an amateur paleontologist who actively promoted paleontology in Europe.

Panphagia (pan-FAYJ-ee-ah)

Age: 231 mya
Size: 3 ft long
Weight: 22 lbs
Location: Argentina
Food: Omnivore

Judging by the shape of its jaws and teeth, Panphagia was able to consume plant material and other animals. That led to its name, which means "eats everything." Scientists found its fossilized remains in 2006, and announced the find in 2009. Panphagia was an early sauropodomorph, a family of dinosaurs transitioning away from being meat-eating theropods toward plant-eating sauropods.

Pantydraco (pan-tee-DRAY-coe)

Age: 210–200 mya
Size: 8 ft long
Weight: 110 lbs
Location: South Wales
Food: Herbivore

This dinosaur came from an oddly named location, the Pantyffynnon Quarry in Wales, United Kingdom. Pantydraco gets the first half of its name from that quarry. "Draco" is a Latin word meaning "dragon." Fossil hunters only found a partial skeleton, and that may have been from a young individual. An adult Pantydraco was probably much larger than the specimen paleontologists discovered. Pantydraco walked on all fours, rearing up on its hind legs like many other herbivores of the time. Some scientists think Pantydraco may have been an omnivore, eating smaller animals or scavenging the dead.

Pisanosaurus (pee-SAHN-oh-sore-us)

Age: 228–216 mya
Size: 4.5 ft long
Weight: 5 lbs
Location: Northern Argentina
Food: Herbivore

This little dinosaur is the earliest known herbivore. It was discovered in 1967, and its jawbone caused immediate debate among paleontologists. Pisanosaurus looked like the bird-hipped dinosaurs in the ornithischian order, but it had body features more like those of the lizard-hipped order called saurischian. It walked on its hind legs, feeding on low-growing vegetation. Rodolfo Casamiquela described and named the dinosaur in 1967. He chose a name meaning "Pisano's lizard" in honor of Argentine paleontologist Juan A. Pisano.

Plateosaurus (PLAT-ee-oh-SORE-us)

Age: 205 mya
Size: 33 ft long
Weight: 3.9 tons
Location: France, Germany, Switzerland, Norway, Greenland
Food: Herbivore

Plateosaurus, or "broad lizard," may have been the first of the massive plant eaters. The number of fossil finds—more than 100 skeletons—in different European countries indicate it may have been one of the more common dinosaurs of its time. Some of those fossils were of several individuals in one location, which may be a sign that it traveled in herds. Plateosaurus walked on all fours, with its back horizontal, then reared up on its hind legs when feeding. Its skull had large holes to make it lighter, a feature common in later large dinosaurs. Plateosaurus's teeth were leaf-shaped and small, suggesting it could shred the thick leaves and stems of Triassic trees.

Riojasaurus (REE-oh-hah-SORE-us)

Age: 210 mya
Size: 33 ft long
Weight: 1,800 lbs
Location: Argentina
Food: Herbivore

Argentine paleontologist José Bonaparte discovered Riojasaurus in 1960, and named it "La Rioja lizard" for the region where he found the first bones. Riojasaurus was a prosauropod, an ancestor of the larger plant-eating sauropods of the Jurassic Period. Its limb bones were among the longest and strongest of any other known herbivores of its kind. A small head, long tail, and long neck made it resemble the larger herbivores to come. It was a slow mover, walking on pillar-like, elephantine legs, and probably traveled in herds for greater protection from predators. Its teeth indicate it fed on conifer tree needles and twigs.

Sanjuansaurus (san-hwan-SORE-us)

Age: 230 mya
Size: 13 ft long
Weight: 550 lbs
Location: Argentina
Food: Carnivore

A partial skeleton, including a leg bone and a piece of jawbone from Sanjuansaurus, came from the same rock formation that revealed Herrerasaurus. The two dinosaurs lived during the same time period. The leg bones indicate that Sanjuansaurus was probably one of the fastest of the predatory dinosaurs in its era. The name means "San Juan lizard" for the city near where its remains lay.

Staurikosaurus (STORE-ick-oh-SORE-us)

Age: 227–221 mya
Size: 7 ft long
Weight: 26 lbs
Location: Southern Brazil
Food: Carnivore

Although small in size, Staurikosaurus had the same basic body shape as its ancestors, including the huge Tyrannosaurs of the Cretaceous Period. It probably chased and ate small lizards and maybe baby dinosaurs. It may also have fed on the kills of larger theropods. Brazilian paleontologist Llewellyn Ivor Price found its bones in the 1940s, but it was not until 30 years later that the dinosaur was named "Southern Cross lizard." The Southern Cross is a star constellation visible in the Southern Hemisphere. Staurikosaurus earned its name because, at the time, few dinosaur fossils had been found in that part of the world.

Compsognathus, from the Jurassic Period

Thecodontosaurus (THEE-co-DON-toe-SORE-us)

Age: 200 mya
Size: 8 ft long
Weight: 22 lbs
Location: British Isles
Food: Herbivore

This plant eater's leaf-shaped, saw-like teeth were unusual enough that scientists Henry Riley and Samuel Stutchbury named it "socket-toothed lizard." Discovered in 1834, it was one of the very early dinosaur finds. In 1975, 11 more specimens were found at Tytherington Quarry in England. Thecodontosaurus had a small head, long legs, and short arms. It could probably graze low plants on all fours, but likely walked and ran on its hind legs.

At the time that Thecodontosaurus lived, England was close to the equator. It had a temperate climate with tropical islands to the west. Paleontologists think that Thecodontosaurus may have inhabited those islands because it is smaller than many other dinosaurs that lived in the same area. Island-based animals often reach smaller sizes because food is less abundant.

Using a Clock

Some elements, such as potassium and argon, experience what is called radioactive decay. Bits of electrically charged particles inside the individual atoms of these elements change in number. These changes occur at a consistent rate over time. Scientists know just how fast these changes happen, so it is much like having a clock. Potassium and argon change very slowly—slow enough that scientists can calculate the age of a fossil by measuring how much those elements in the fossils changed or decayed. This kind of clock is accurate enough to measure a fossil or rock billions of years old.

DIGGING DEEPER

The Bone Wars

In the mid- to late-1800s, the competitive spirit of finding new dinosaur fossils took a strange twist. Two paleontologists—Edward Drinker Cope and Othniel C. Marsh—took the competition between them to all new levels.

The two men met in Germany when Cope went there to study natural history and Marsh was a graduate student. They quickly developed a friendship, and it continued when both returned to the United States. But a short time later, their relationship soured. Two incidents occurred in 1868 that seemed to ignite the war between Cope and Marsh.

Cope was working to unearth fossils in a rich dinosaur quarry in New Jersey. He showed Marsh around the area, but unknown to Cope, Marsh was working a deal with the owner of the quarry. He convinced the owner to send the new fossil finds to him at Yale University instead of to Cope.

That same year, Cope was so pleased with one of his discoveries, Elasmosaurus, that he rushed to get his information published in a scientific journal. In his haste, Cope placed the head on the wrong end of the dinosaur. Marsh was quick to point out the problem, which was verified by another paleontologist. In his embarrassment, Cope tried unsuccessfully to collect and destroy every copy of the journal in which his paper was published.

Over the next 20 years, things just got worse and worse between the two men. Both had plenty of money. Cope was from a wealthy family, and Marsh inherited a great sum from a rich uncle, industrialist George Peabody. Their finances fueled their fossil exploration, but it also fed their desire to one up the other person.

Stories of foul deeds include bribes paid to workers of the other person, covering and disguising digs, littering a site with confusing bone fragments to throw off the other paleontologist and spying. Both men are also suspected of dynamiting their own dinosaur digs and destroying the fossils within rather than letting their competitor claim the site.

Edward Drinker Cope, c. 1890

Othniel Charles Marsh,
c. 1870

Both men raced to find the next dinosaur, and hurried to get their findings known across the world. Cope was so concerned to have his papers published, that he bought *The American Naturalist* journal just to ensure that he did. The following year, he published 76 scientific papers about his discoveries.

One of Marsh's discoveries was a nearly complete skeleton of an Apatosaurus. However, the skull was missing. That did not stop him from getting the find displayed. He simply attached a skull from a different dinosaur, possibly a Camarasaurus. Later, a similar dinosaur emerged from one of Marsh's digs, this one complete with a skull. Thinking he had found a new species, he named that one Brontosaurus. As it turned out, it was another Apatosaurus. The mistake was not caught until nearly 20 years later. Brontosaurus was dropped and Apatosaurus was assigned to both finds.

By the time both men died, they had burned through their fortunes, mostly in an effort to outdo their rival. Cope was nearly bankrupt when he died in 1897. Marsh had but $186 left to his name when he died 2 years later.

Despite the drama between these two men, the world was richer for the attention drawn to dinosaurs and the science of paleontology. More than 140 new dinosaur species were discovered and documented. The public, as curious about the ongoing feud as they were the science, became much more aware of the world millions of years before their own time.

Magnetic Rocks

When we open a compass, we know exactly which way north is because the needle always points in that direction. The Earth is like a great big magnet. But if we had a compass and traveled back in time, we would find that the needle sometimes pointed north, and it sometimes pointed south. That is because the Earth's magnet sometimes changed polarity. Scientists know when those polarity changes occurred, so they can measure a fossil's age by how magnetic particles in the rock are lined up.

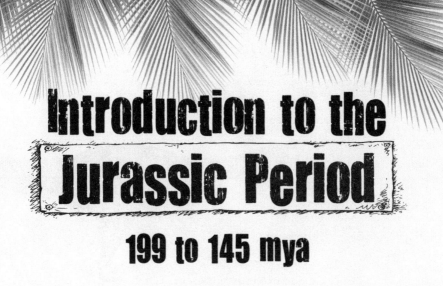

Introduction to the Jurassic Period

199 to 145 mya

Another mass extinction marked the end of the Triassic Period and the beginning of the Jurassic Period. This one was not as severe as the extinction that occurred near the beginning of the Triassic. Still, nearly three-fourths of all life on land and in the oceans died.

Earthquakes and volcanoes probably occurred often, and over several million years, as the great land mass of Pangaea broke apart into two new continents: Laurasia to the north and Gondwana to the south. The upheaval caused by volcanic ash, dust, and gases may have contributed to a change in climate that killed great numbers of animals.

A new, shallow sea filled the space between the two new land masses. Eventually, rain could reach areas that were once arid desert. Temperatures cooled and deserts grew lush with vegetation. Plants had not yet adapted flowers or fruits, but horsetails, ferns, conifer trees, and cycads were plentiful along the Jurassic landscape.

Throughout the Triassic and Jurassic Periods, the moon orbited a little closer to Earth than it does today. That made it look bigger in the sky, and the nights were a little brighter because the moon reflected more sunlight.

Many scientists believe that the disappearance of other animal species that once competed with dinosaurs, along with less extreme habitats and plenty of food, allowed dinosaurs to flourish. As the Jurassic Period moved forward, the great plant eaters, such as Apatosaurus, Brachiosaurus, and Diplodocus emerged. These were the sauropods, huge beasts that stood on all fours while reaching treetops using their long necks. Fierce predators, such as Allosaurus and Megalosaurus, preyed on other dinosaurs during Jurassic times.

Named for the Jura Mountains along the border between France and Switzerland, the Jurassic Period was when dinosaurs rose to rule the world. They would do so for the next 130 million years.

Aardonyx (ar-DON-ix)

Age: 199–196 mya
Size: 23 ft long
Weight: 1,100 lbs
Location: South Africa
Food: Herbivore

First discovered in 2009, Aardonyx fits into a gap that once existed in the evolution of dinosaurs. Its bones and muscles, the way it stood, and how it ate places it between the small prosauropods of the Triassic Period and the massive sauropods of the later Jurassic period. Like sauropods, it had a long tail and a small head. However, it walked on two legs like prosauropods. It had stronger forearms than most prosauropods, and the bones in those arms were beginning to get less flexible, which is important when supporting huge weight. It could also open its mouth wider than a prosauropod, allowing Aardonyx to pull off leaves in large bites instead of picking them a little at a time. This dinosaur's name means "earth claw," which describes the hard iron ore that surrounded the fossil's toes. That ore made it difficult for scientists to free the toe bones.

Agilisaurus (ah-JILL-oh-sore-us)

Age: 164–161 mya
Size: 4 ft long
Weight: 33 lbs
Location: Sichuan Province, China
Food: Herbivore

As the name suggests, Agilisaurus was agile and had graceful movements. It was also very quick, and it could run away from danger at high speeds using its long hind legs. Agilisaurus may have stood on four legs when eating low growing vegetation, such as ferns. A complete skeleton emerged from a dig in China's Dashanpu Quarry, where many other dinosaur bones have been found.

Allosaurus (AL-oh-SORE-us)

Age: 155–150 mya
Size: 28 ft long
Weight: 1.6 tons
Location: USA: Colorado, Montana, New Mexico, Oklahoma, South Dakota, Utah, Wyoming
Food: Carnivore

Allosaurus relied on its excellent hearing and keen sense of smell to locate its prey. When attacking, many paleontologists believe Allosaurus hid, then surprised victims by jumping at them in an ambush. An S-shaped neck and strong hind legs gave Allosaurus incredible strength to carry out such attacks. Powerful arms with 10-inch-long claws for ripping and tearing along with massive jaws on a head 3 feet long made quick work of a meal. Allosaurus could push its jaw outward, so it could swallow large chunks of meat. Its 70 teeth, some as long as 4 inches, were serrated like a steak knife. A single Allosaurus was a fearsome predator, but some scientists suggest it may also have hunted in packs. A large number of sauropod bones have scrapes and other damage that fit marks made by Allosaurus teeth.

Othniel C. Marsh named Allosaurus, which means "other lizard," in 1877. The first complete skeleton emerged from a site in Colorado. Not long after, Utah's Cleveland-Lloyd Dinosaur Quarry yielded 60 more individuals. Specimens fall into all age groups, young and old. The number of finds indicates that Allosaurus was abundant across what would become the American West and Midwest.

Ammosaurus (AM-oh-sore-us)

Age: 189–176 mya
Size: 16 ft long
Weight: 485 lbs
Location: USA: New England
Food: Omnivore

Workers building a bridge in Manchester, CT, during the late 1800s used a large chunk of sandstone carved from a nearby quarry. As more material was excavated from that quarry, workers discovered the rear half of a plant-eating dinosaur. The rest of the skeleton was missing. The dinosaur was named "sand lizard" because of the sandstone that preserved its bones.

In 1969, that 19th-century bridge was demolished to make way for other structures. That's when workers found the other half of the Ammosaurus skeleton buried in the sandstone chunk from years earlier. At last, scientists were able to get a better idea of what the animal looked like, how it could walk—on two legs or on all fours—and what its diet may have included.

Anchiornis (an-chee-ORE-nis)

Age: 160–155 mya
Size: 13 in long
Weight: 4 oz
Location: China
Food: Insectivore

Its name means "near bird," and Anchiornis certainly was. Covered in distinct feathers and with a tiny, light frame, Anchiornis looked much like a bird. Scientists still consider this specimen a dinosaur, however, because its feathers were not placed to suggest it could fly. At best, it may have glided from tree to tree. Anchiornis also had wrist bones that looked much like those found in birds. One of the first dinosaurs that scientists could study for color, Anchiornis had black feathers, with white stripes. Its head was speckled black and red, and it sported a crest of head feathers that resembled a Mohawk haircut. The crest was a reddish-orange.

Anchisaurus (ankey-SORE-us)

Age: 200 mya
Size: 8 ft long
Weight: 60 lbs
Location: USA: Connecticut, Massachusetts
Food: Herbivore

One of the first dinosaurs found in North America. Anchisaurus was discovered in a block of sandstone from the same quarry as Ammosaurus. This dinosaur was similar in many ways to Ammosaurus, and paleontologists debated for years whether they were actually the same dinosaur. While many agree that Ammosaurus is really the same as Anchisaurus, others point out subtle differences in the pelvis and other bones.

Apatosaurus (a-PAT-oh-SORE-us)

Age: 154–150 mya
Size: 75 ft long
Weight: 26.5 tons
Location: USA: Colorado, Utah, Oklahoma, Wyoming, Mexico
Food: Herbivore

Apatosaurus was a huge plant eater with a very long tail and neck. The tail contained 82 bones, and it was capable of being flicked like a whip. Very likely, this was a defensive tool for Apatosaurus, one that could inflict serious and even fatal injury to predators.

Some scientists argue that this dinosaur's neck was not flexible enough for it to reach into treetops. They imagine Apatosaurus knocking down entire trees, then stripping them of leaves and shoots while on the ground. Other paleontologists disagree, stating the neck shows plenty of flexibility for browsing high treetops. This dinosaur probably traveled in herds along riverbanks lined with forests and woodlands. It had small jaws, so it likely had to eat constantly, only stopping long enough to cool itself in rivers or take short naps.

Archaeopteryx (ar-key-OP-ter-ix)

Age: 150 mya
Size: 1.5 ft long
Weight: 2 lbs
Location: Germany
Food: Carnivore

Recognized as the oldest known member of the bird family, Archaeopteryx amazed scientists studying it after the first discovery in 1861. The animal looked like a cross between a dinosaur and a bird. Fossil remains showed that the wings and tail were fully feathered, but it had dinosaur-like claws on its hands and jaws lined with teeth instead of a beak. Its flight feathers were long, but Archaeopteryx was without the powerful muscles needed for flying. It probably glided from one tree to the next, much like a modern flying squirrel.

At the time when Archaeopteryx lived, its part of Europe had a tropical climate. Land masses were made up of a series of islands in a warm sea. As a result, scientists think Archaeopteryx's diet consisted of insects, small reptiles, and possibly fish. Some scientists also speculate that Archaeopteryx could swim.

Aviatyrannis (AY-vee-ah-tie-RAN-us)

Age: 155–150 mya
Size: 3 ft long
Weight: 11 lbs
Location: Portugal
Food: Carnivore

Just a few hip bone fragments were all that were found of this dinosaur, first described in 2003. Aviatyrannis was an ancestor of the great tyrannosaurs that would arrive about 80 million years later, but it did not resemble them in size. Small and very light, Aviatyrannis's name means "tyrant's grandmother," referring to the massive Tyrannosaurus rex of the Cretaceous period. The discovery of Aviatyrannis bones occurred in an old coalmine in an area that was a wooded island during the Jurassic Period.

Barapasaurus (buh-RAH-pah-SORE-us)

Age: 189–176 mya
Size: 59 ft long
Weight: 20 tons
Location: India
Food: Herbivore

One of the earliest sauropods, Barapasaurus appeared near the beginning of the Jurassic Period. A complete skull has yet to be found, but several sharp teeth show saw-like edges, an unusual characteristic in sauropods. Its tail was nearly twice as long as its neck, and it stood on all fours. Barapasaurus's legs were thick and sturdy, and its name means "big-legged lizard." Its fossilized remains were unearthed in 1959 and described in 1975, but it was not until 2010 that paleontologists finally finished sifting through all 300 bones from this animal, describing them in greater detail.

Barosaurus (BARE-oh-SORE-us)

Age: 150 mya
Size: 75–89 ft long
Weight: 44 tons
Location: Tanzania; USA: South Dakota, Utah
Food: Herbivore

Its name means "heavy lizard," and Barosaurus was among the largest of all dinosaurs. It would have stood around 50 feet tall, close to the size of a 5-story building. Some of the vertebrae were 3 feet long, but they were hollow bones to save weight. Otherwise, Barosaurus's neck would have been too hard to raise.

Brachiosaurus (brack-ee-oh-SORE-us)

Age: 153 mya

Size: 82 ft long

Weight: 27.5 tons

Location: USA: Colorado

Food: Herbivore

The "arm lizard" was shaped very much like a giraffe, but it could reach about 3 times higher than giraffes. Huge and hungry, scientists estimate a single Brachiosaurus had to eat around 260 pounds of leaves every day in order to keep its body functioning. Although it could feed at heights of 50 feet, Brachiosaurus was unable to rear up on its hind legs in order to reach higher tree limbs. That's because more than half of its weight was toward its front.

Brachytrachelopan (BRACK-ee-tra-KEL-oh-pan)

Age: 150–145 mya

Size: 33 ft long

Weight: 5.4 tons

Location: Argentina

Food: Herbivore

From its shoulders to its tail, Brachytrachelopan looked much like a typical sauropod. It stood on all fours and it had a long tail. But its neck was much shorter than those of its relatives. In fact, its name means "short-necked pan." This dinosaur find was announced in 2005, with researchers pointing out that the unusual neck helped Brachytrachelopan browse low-growing plants. The way its bones were constructed, Brachytrachelopan would not have been able to lift its head past horizontal.

Comparing Fossils to Rock

If you ride in a car along a highway, you might come across places where a section of hill was removed and the road built. You can see different layers of colors in the exposed rock. Geologists understand how and when each layer was deposited. These layers provide a consistent way to know the age of the rocks. Comparing the rock layer to the fossils it contains gives a good idea of the age of those fossils.

Camarasaurus (KAM-ah-ra-SORE-us)

Age: 185–145 mya

Size: 59 ft long

Weight: 22.6 tons

Location: USA: Colorado, Utah, Wyoming; Portugal

Food: Herbivore

Large eye openings suggest that Camarasaurus had excellent vision. Scientists also think it had a good sense of smell. Camarasaurus had lots of openings in its vertebrae, which helped it save weight. In fact, Edward Drinker Cope named this dinosaur Camarasaurus after its discovery in 1877. Camarasaurus means "chambered lizard." Some hollowed bones had air chambers that connected to this dinosaur's lungs. That could mean it had a way of creating loud noises for signaling other dinosaurs. Camarasaurus's spoon-shaped teeth were strong, suggesting it may have eaten tough branches as well as leaves, and chewed them instead of swallowing them whole.

Many fossils have been found in the western United States, some in large groups, which probably mean this dinosaur traveled in herds. Camarasaurus was likely the most common herbivore of the late Jurassic Period.

Camptosaurus (CAMP-toe-SORE-us)

Age: 150 mya
Size: 16 ft long
Weight: 1,100 lbs
Location: USA: Wyoming
Food: Herbivore

Camptosaurus, which means "bent lizard," had a thumb spike among its five fingers. Because this dinosaur was relatively small, the spike was probably not used to defend itself. Instead, it may have helped strip trees, or hold them while it consumed the leaves. Usually plodding along on all fours, Camptosaurus could rear up on its hind legs and run away from danger at speeds of up to 15 mph.

Camptosaurus's head was shaped like that of a horse, and its beak was loaded with teeth. The wear and tear on its teeth indicates that its diet consisted of tough vegetation, such as thick plants and twigs.

Ceratosaurus (SERR-at-oh-SORE-us)

Age: 153–148 mya
Size: 23 ft long
Weight: 1,500 lbs
Location: USA: Colorado, Wyoming; Tanzania
Food: Carnivore

This "horned lizard" had bony ridges on its head, along its back, and at the end of its tail. It also sported a short horn on its head as well as some bony knobs on its upper body, including one above each eye. Ceratosaurus preyed on reptiles and on smaller dinosaurs that lived in the tree-covered plains on which it roamed. Some paleontologists think Ceratosaurus may also have eaten aquatic animals because of its swampy environment.

Ceratosaurus had a heavy tail that could only waggle at the very end because most of its tailbones were stiff. The way its limbs were built shows that Ceratosaurus could run in bursts of great speed in order to chase down its prey. Its jaws were large and it had curved, blade-like fangs.

Cetiosauriscus (SEE-tee-oh-sore-ISS-cuss)

Age: 163 mya
Size: 49 ft long
Weight: 3.9 tons
Location: England
Food: Herbivore

German paleontologist Friedrich von Huene named Cetiosauriscus in 1927. The name means "like the whale-like lizard," because von Huene noted that Cetiosauriscus was very similar to Cetiosaurus, the "whale-like lizard." Some of the fossils had originally been classified as belonging to Cetiosaurus before a series of vertebrae and a front leg were reclassified into a new genus.

Cetiosaurus (SEE-tee-oh-SORE-us)

Age: 180–170 mya
Size: 59 ft long
Weight: 26.6 tons
Location: England, Morocco
Food: Herbivore

Cetiosaurus lived in herds along what was once a sea in Jurassic England. In 1869, fossil hunters unearthed a nearly complete skeleton from rocks near Oxfordshire, England. Similar bones found earlier were thought to be from whales or animals related to crocodiles. Thomas Henry Huxley identified those early remains as belonging to a dinosaur, and the name he gave it means "whale-like lizard."

Cetiosaurus had a heavy, solid backbone rather than the hollow kind its descendants would develop. Its limbs looked like those of modern elephants, and its feet had thick pads at the toes. Cetiosaurus's head was blunt, its mouth filled with spoon-shaped teeth suitable for a diet of ferns and trees.

Chialingosaurus (jah-LING-oh SORE-us)

Age: 159–142 mya
Size: 13 ft long
Weight: 500 lbs
Location: China
Food: Herbivore

Chialingosaurus was the first dinosaur of the stegosaur family that was found in China. It was smaller and thinner looking than the stegosaurs that would emerge later. Chialingosaurus had two parallel rows of small plates and spikes along its back and tail. Its skull was narrow with teeth spaced apart. It fed on low-growing vegetation, but it did have tail vertebrae that indicated it could rear up and stand on its hind legs. In 1959, a partial skeleton emerged near the Jialing River, giving Chialingosaurus its name.

Compsognathus (COMP-sog-NAYTH-us)

Age: 150 mya
Size: 4 ft long
Weight: 5.5 lbs
Location: France, Southern Germany
Food: Carnivore

The first Compsognathus fossil emerged in 1861 and, because it wasn't very big, experts at the time didn't even think it was a dinosaur. All of the other dinosaurs found up to that time were massive beasts. This find showed that dinosaurs existed in all different sizes.

Compsognathus lived in what was a group of islands where Western Europe is now. There it hunted small animals. One of the fossils had the remains of a final meal: a lizard. Compsognathus was built much like modern birds, although it could not fly. Its head was narrow and it drew to a point, giving rise to its name, which means "dainty jaw." It had a long neck and a mouthful of curved, sharp teeth. Compsognathus had large eyes, and a tail that made up more than half of its body length. Its short arms had two fingers and claws. The body was very light, so Compsognathus was probably a swift runner.

Condorraptor (CON-door-rap-tore)

Age: 164 mya
Size: 15 ft long
Weight: 440 lbs
Location: Southern Argentina
Food: Carnivore

Hipólito Currumil, an Argentinian farmer, found a single bone in a field near the village of Cerro Condor. It proved to be an arm bone called a tibia. Paleontologist Oliver Rauhut identified the bone as belonging to a new dinosaur, a small predator. A near complete skeleton emerged in 2007. Its joints were still intact and they revealed Condorraptor as a swift-running meat eater.

Cryolophosaurus (CRY-oh-LOFF-oh-SORE-us)

Age: 190 mya
Size: 21 ft long
Weight: 1,025 lbs
Location: Antarctica: Mount Kirkpatrick
Food: Carnivore

Cryolophosaurus was the first dinosaur found in Antarctica. Its remains were lying 13,000 feet up a mountainside. At the time that it lived, Antarctica was hundreds of miles farther north, so its climate was warmer. The area was covered by a vast forest that likely supported plant-eating dinosaurs, flying pterosaurs, and mammal-like reptiles, all of which probably made up Cryolophosaurus's diet.

Cryolophosaurus was nicknamed "Elvisaurus" because it had an odd crest atop its head. The nickname refers to a hairstyle worn by singer Elvis Presley. Its real name, however, means "frozen crested lizard." The crest was facing forward and it was mounted just above the eyes.

Datousaurus (DAT-oo-SORE-us)

Age: 180 mya

Size: 33 ft long

Weight: 4.4 tons

Location: China

Food: Herbivore

Two partial skeletons, one with a partial skull, came from Dashanpu Quarry in China. That quarry has been rich with fossilized dinosaur bones. Datousaurus, which means "chieftain lizard," was one of the few sauropods of its time as most dinosaurs in that family came later in the Jurassic Period. Datousaurus had a long neck and an unusually heavy head.

Dicraeosaurus (DIE-cray-oh-SORE-us)

Age: 150 mya

Size: 39 ft long

Weight: 5.5 tons

Location: Tanzania

Food: Herbivore

The name means "two-forked lizard," referring to the series of bony spines along its backbone. Some paleontologists speculate that the spines may have been covered with skin, forming a sail. Dicraeosaurus had a shorter neck than other sauropods, suggesting it ate low-growing vegetation. Its tail was also shorter for balance, but it was unlikely Dicraeosaurus used its tail as a defensive whip.

Dilophosaurus (die-LOAF-oh-SORE-us)

Age: 195 mya
Size: 23 ft long
Weight: 900 lbs
Location: USA: Arizona
Food: Carnivore

Dilophosaurus had bony crests that looked like half circles, one on each side of its skull. The crests may have been used to attract mates, or for cooling and they gave Dilophosaurus its name, which means "double-crested lizard." Dilophosaurus earned its name 28 years after Jesse Williams, a Navajo Indian, led researchers to the original fossil find in 1942. The bones were first thought to belong to a Megalosaurus before close examination revealed that the crests had broken.

In the movie *Jurassic Park*, Dilophosaurus appears smaller and with the ability to spit poison. At 23 feet, the real Dilophosaurus was much larger. Also, no dinosaur is known to have been venomous.

Diplodocus (DIP-low-DOCK-us)

Age: 154–150 mya
Size: 89 ft long
Weight: 17.7 tons
Location: USA: Colorado, Utah, Wyoming
Food: Herbivore

One of the longest dinosaurs ever discovered, Diplodocus had 15 vertebrae in its long, snaky neck and 70 to 80 vertebrae in its even longer tail. The tail narrowed to a flexible, whip-like tip. Samuel Wilson, a fossil hunter, discovered the first partial skeleton in Colorado in 1877. Wyoming yielded the first good skeletal remains 22 years later. In 1990, a fossilized Diplodocus skin impression showed a row of spines on the animal's tail. These may have run along its back all the way up to its neck.

Diplodocus could have reared up on its hind legs while using its tail as a tripod. This would enable it to reach leaves at the very tops of trees. Its teeth were arranged in such a way that it could strip all of the leaves from a branch rather than nibbling away at clumps of leaves. Without back teeth, Diplodocus could not chew, so it swallowed vegetation whole and let its muscular stomach grind the material to a pulp. Once Diplodocus ate everything it could in one area, it moved on to new locations.

Diplodocus's name means "double beam," and it describes the long bones in its tail. Diplodocus could swing its tail with lightning speed, producing a crack just like that of a whip. This was probably a very useful defense mechanism as the tail could deliver serious, maybe even fatal blows to predators. Diplodocus also had a single claw on its elephant-like feet, perhaps as a second means of defense.

Drinker (DRINK-er)

Age: 155 mya
Size: 6.5 ft
Weight: 44 lbs
Location: USA: Wyoming
Food: Herbivore

Drinker was a light and speedy dinosaur. It was named by Peter Galton and Robert Bakker in honor of early fossil hunter Edward Drinker Cope. Drinker had to swiftly dodge between the feet of massive sauropods as it scurried about, pecking away at low growing vegetation. Its toes were spread out, suggesting that it may have lived where the ground was soft, such as in a swamp. This dinosaur was similar in many ways to Othnielosaurus.

Dryosaurus (DRAY-oh-SORE-us)

Age: 155–145 mya
Size: 10 ft long
Weight: 2,000 pounds
Location: North America, Europe, East Africa
Food: Herbivore

Named the "oak lizard" for its teeth, which were shaped like oak leaves and ideal for grinding the leaves it consumed. Dryosaurus had a parrot-like beak. It was a swift runner on powerful, lightweight but long legs. A stiff tail gave Dryosaurus balance as it moved. It also had five fingers on each hand for grasping food.

Dubreuillosaurus (due-BROY-oh-SORE-us)

Age: 170 mya
Size: 26 ft long
Weight: 1,500 lbs
Location: France
Food: Carnivore

A skull and some ribs were the only pieces found of a Dubreuillosaurus skeleton. The remains came from an abandoned quarry in France. Scientists returned to the site later to see what else they could find, but the quarry had reopened and they discovered only smashed fossil remnants. French paleontologist Ronan Allain took on the tough task of sorting and analyzing bone fragments, which he described in 2005. Dubreuillosaurus was named in 2002, honoring the Dubreuill family.

The dinosaur had a very long but shallow skull that was almost three times longer than it was tall. The stout, bulky dinosaur hunted what were then coastal mangroves in Laurasia. Its skull structure and its large fangs were suited for catching fish from the swamp waters where it roamed.

Eoabelisaurus (EE-oh-ay-BELL-ih-SORE-us)

Age: 176–168 mya
Size: 20 ft long
Weight: 1,980 lbs
Location: Argentina
Food: Carnivore

Abelisaurs were a group of dinosaurs with similar traits, and Eoabelisaurus was among the first of that group to appear. As a result, its name means "dawn abelisaur." Eoabelisaurus had a short skull and small arms with tiny hands. It was named in 2002 by paleontologists Diego Pol and Oliver Rauhut, who noted in their description that they found it surprising no such dinosaurs were uncovered in Europe. At that point in Jurassic times, Gondwana had not yet split into continents. The two scientists speculate that some barrier—perhaps a formidable desert—lay in the way.

Epidexipteryx (EPP-ee-dex-IP-ter-ix)

Age: 168–160 mya
Size: 1 foot long
Weight: .5 lbs
Location: Mongolia
Food: Possibly an insectivore

A small and odd-looking creature's fossil remains was discovered in 2008. This dinosaur was covered in a fluffy down. It had four long tail feathers that were likely ornamental, as the animal could not fly. Epidexipteryx was very similar in appearance to modern birds. Fossil impressions show definite marks left behind by feathers, although Epidexipteryx existed millions of years before its descendants could fly. Epidexipteryx also had small claws and a third finger. Paleontologists think those may have aided the dinosaur in probing for beetle grubs as it maneuvered up trees.

Europasaurus (you-ROPE-ah-SORE-us)

Age: 155–150 mya
Size: 20 ft long
Weight: 1,100 lbs
Location: Germany
Food: Herbivore

Compared to the huge sauropods of the era, Europasaurus was tiny. It lived in an area that was a series of small islands at the time. Islands often have less resources than larger land masses, so animals evolve in smaller sizes. This trait is called "island dwarfism." A closer study of the fossilized bones revealed that Europasaurus grew far more slowly than its gigantic sauropod cousins. It takes its name from the continent of Europe.

Eustreptospondylus (you-STREP-toe-SPON-dill-us)

Age: 165 mya

Size: 23 ft long
Weight: 485 lbs
Location: England:
Buckinghamshire, Oxfordshire
Food: Carnivore

This hunter was built lightly for speed. It had a short spine, and its name means "well-curved vertebrae," referring to its backbone. Like many theropods, Eustreptospondylus had short arms, a powerful jaw, and sharp teeth.

Fruitadens (FROOT-ah-dens)

Age: 150 mya
Size: 2.5 ft long
Weight: 1.7 lbs
Location: USA: Colorado
Food: Omnivore

Despite its name, Fruitadens did not eat fruit. Mostly because plants did not develop fruit or flowers until millions of years later during the Cretaceous Period. Fruitadens takes its name from the Colorado town of Fruita, where its fossilized remains emerged from sandstone during the 1970s and 1980s. Its mix of teeth—sharp front canines for tearing meat and blunted pegs for grinding and chewing plant material—suggest that Fruitadens ate most anything it could find. This animal was lean and ran on its hind legs.

4" TALL

Jurassic

Gargoyleosaurus (gar-GOY-lee-oh-SORE-us)

Age: 155–150 mya
Size: 10 ft long
Weight: 9 tons
Location: USA: Wyoming
Food: Herbivore

A predator's only chance at making a meal of Gargoyleosaurus would be to flip the little creature on its back. Gargoyleosaurus was so heavily armored that most predators' teeth would break trying to penetrate its body. It had hollow plates protecting its back and sides. It also had spikes on its sides to further discourage an attack.

Gargoyleosaurus was an ankylosaur, but it had straight nostrils rather than the looping ones found in other dinosaurs in this group. Like many other ankylosaurs, Gargoyleosaurus was squat and slow moving, its armor the only means of defense at its disposal.

Gargoyleosaurus was first described in 1998, and it was named for the resemblance between its skull and those portrayed on gothic stone gargoyles that designers sometimes perched on buildings.

Gasosaurus (GAS-oh-SORE-us)

Age: 168–161 mya
Size: 11.5 ft long
Weight: 440 lbs
Location: China
Food: Carnivore

A Chinese gas mining company accidentally discovered a few scattered bones, and no skull, while blasting rocks with dynamite. The animal was named "gas lizard" because of the way it was found. Even though little fossilized remains emerged, paleontologists still managed to determine that Gasosaurus was a theropod. In 2014, there were reports of a 160-million-year-old Gasosaurus egg that accidentally hatched when a museum heating system failed. This was a hoax that fooled many people. Like fossilized bones, dinosaur eggs were long ago converted to stone, with no chance of hatching.

Giraffatitan (ji-RAFF-oh-tie-tan)

Age: 155–145 mya
Size: 73 ft long
Weight: 22.6 tons
Location: Tanzania
Food: Herbivore

A little smaller, but otherwise very similar to Brachiosaurus, a Giraffatitan could consume an estimated 260 pounds of plant material every day. When Werner Janensch discovered the bones in Tanzania in 1914, he thought he had found an African species of the Brachiosaurus that Elmer Riggs had named in 1900. Janensch called his find Brachiosaurus brancai. But in 1988, paleontologist Gregory Paul realized the dinosaurs were actually two completely different animals, and he named Janensch's discovery Giraffatitan. In 2009, paleontologist Mike Taylor described 26 differences between the bones of Brachiosaurs and those of Giraffatitan.

Guanlong (GWON-long)

Age: 160 mya
Size: 11.5 ft long
Weight: 275 lbs
Location: China: Junggar Basin
Food: Carnivore

Guanlong means "crowned dragon," a name earned because of the hollow crest that extended from its nose to the back of its head. The crest was probably only for display, so it may have been richly colored. Discovered in 1996, Guanlong was an early relative of the great tyrannosaurs of the Cretaceous Period. It had three fingers on each hand, and those were long and strong. Guanlong was closely related to feathered dinosaurs, and it may have worn a layer of fluffy down itself.

Haplocheirus (HAP-low-KEER-us)

Age: 160 mya
Size: 7 ft long
Weight: 55 lbs
Location: China
Food: Carnivore

Archaeopteryx is widely recognized as the first known bird, but Haplocheirus, which lived 15 million years earlier than Archaeopteryx, looked very much like a bird itself. Despite its feathered body, Haplocheirus only shared one common ancestor with birds. Haplocheirus had three strong fingers on each hand, with the middle one especially long. It may have used those fingers to capture prey and hold it in its grasp. These hands were impressive enough that Haplocheirus was named "simple skillful hand."

Finding Dinosaur Bones

Finding dinosaur fossils requires a mix of skill and luck, but it does not matter how old you are or whether you are a paleontologist. Many dinosaur discoveries were made by people who happened to find something that did not look quite right. Others, like 14-year-old Wes Linster, made important discoveries while hunting fossils in national parks. Wes found the skeleton of a new dinosaur genus, Bambiraptor.

The skill part comes in knowing where to look. In the United States, for example, the Midwestern states were part of a sea throughout much of the Mesozoic Era. In most of the northeastern states, the underlying rocks are too old for dinosaurs, while in the southeast, rocks are too young. With some exceptions, most dinosaur finds in the U.S. have been in the western states—the Dakotas, Montana, Wyoming, Colorado, Utah, Arizona, Texas, Oklahoma, and a few others. Some emerged in Connecticut and Massachusetts and a few more in other states.

Heterodontosaurus (het-er-oh-DON-toe-SORE-us)

Age: 205 mya
Size: 4 ft long
Weight: 5.5 lbs
Location: South Africa, Lesotho
Food: Herbivore

Ornithopod was a group of dinosaurs with three long toes on each foot, each facing forward. Heterodontosaurus was one of the earliest ornithopods, and it was among the smallest of the group. With three different types of teeth, it earned the name "different-toothed lizard." Alfred Crompton and Alan Charig assigned the name in 1962. Scientists discovered a complete skeleton in 1976. Heterodontosaurus was a fast runner, and it could maneuver quickly. It lived in what was a near desert in what is now South Africa.

Could You Discover a Dinosaur?

Depending on where you live, it is possible that dinosaur bones lay in deep rocks beneath your house, in your yard, or on your land. Sometimes, wind and erosion reveal fossils at the surface, or bone fragments may surface and lead to discoveries deeper underground. Most of the time, the more complete fossilized remains of dinosaurs must be located by digging.

Should you find a fossil while hunting on federal or state land, you will need to give it to a state or federal agency. But if you find one on land you own, it is yours to keep and do with what you would like. You could put it in your room, give it to a museum or university, or sell it.

Huayangosaurus (HWAH-YANG-oh-SORE-us)

Age: 165 mya
Size: 13 ft long
Weight: 1 ton
Location: China
Food: Herbivore

Huayangosaurus is an early stegosaur, a group of dinosaurs with spikes and spiky plates running their backs. Unlike its descendants, Huayangosaurus had four legs of nearly equal length. Later stegosaurs had front legs that were slightly shorter than their hind legs. Huayangosaurus's snout was also broader than later stegosaurs. The name means "lizard from Huayang."

Janenschia (yan-ENSH-ee-ah)

Age: 154–151 mya
Size: 65 ft long
Weight: 9.8 tons
Location: Tanzania
Food: Herbivore

Named for German paleontologist Werner Janensch, this large sauropod was an ancestor of the huge titanosaurs yet to come. It had a long neck and tail, and it walked on four thick legs. The rear feet were equipped with claws. Only a single, partial skeleton was found. Unlike many other sauropods, no Janenschia bone yards have ever been uncovered. That may mean Janenschia was a solitary animal.

Like many of the other large sauropods, Janenschia may have had high blood pressure. A huge heart, wide blood vessels, and valves to prevent blood from flowing backward may have made up Janenschia's circulatory system. In order for blood to reach as high as its head, its blood pressure had to have exceeded 400 mm of mercury, which is about 3–4 times that of an average human.

Jobaria (joe-BAR-ee-ah)

Age: 164–161 mya
Size: 53 ft long
Weight: 15.7 tons
Location: Northern Africa
Food: Herbivore

Paleontologist Paul Sereno and his team discovered an almost complete skeleton of this dinosaur in 1997. Area tribespeople took Sereno and his group to a spot where they said laid the old bones of a mythical beast they named Jobar. The dinosaur's name means "big nose" and it describes Jobaria's large snout.

This part of Africa was woodland during the Jurassic Period, and Jobaria wandered among the lush greens, sometimes rearing up to reach leaves in some of the tallest branches. Its tail was short and its vertebrae simple compared to those features on the even larger herbivores that appeared later.

Juravenator (JURE-a-ven-AY-tore)

Age: 152 mya
Size: 2 ft long
Weight: 3.3 lbs
Location: Germany
Food: Carnivore

This dino's name comes from the Jura Mountains where its skeleton first emerged. The only known specimen was a juvenile. A notch on its jaw demonstrated that Juravenator was good at grabbing fish.

Scientists conducted research and experiments between 2010 and 2011 that suggested that the bones surrounding Juravenator's eyes were typical of animals that could see well in low light. That would have made Juravenator a good nocturnal hunter. The experiments showed that Juravenator left faint impressions of patchy feathers along with a rough, scaly skin.

Kentrosaurus (KEN-troh-SORE-us)

Age: 156–150 mya
Size: 16 ft long
Weight: 1 ton
Location: Tanzania
Food: Herbivore

Scientists were able to complete two entire skeletons from more than 900 bones collected in 1900 near where a prehistoric river emptied into an ocean. Kentrosaurus had a short neck and forearms that were shorter than its hind legs. Those characteristics suggest it ate low-growing vegetation as it moved about on all fours.

A stegosaur, Kentrosaurus also had seven pairs of bony plates extending from its neck and shoulder regions. But it earned its name, which means "spiky lizard" from the flat spines on its back and tail. Kentrosaurus used eight pairs—five along the tail and three along its back—of these flat spines as a means of defense. It could back into its enemies' tails first, or swing its tail at predators.

Kotasaurus (Koh-ta-SORE-us)

Age: 196–183 mya
Size: 30 ft long
Weight: 2.4 tons
Location: Southeast India
Food: Herbivore

A heavy body, long tail, and long neck made Kotasaurus one of the earliest known sauropods. Its legs suggest it kept its body horizontal with the ground as it browsed plant material. The skeletal remains were mixed together in what used to be a riverbed. That fueled scientists' theory that a Kotasaurus herd drowned, maybe in a flash flood, and its collection of bones was carried downstream to where paleontologists discovered them.

Lufengosaurus (loo-FENG-oh-SORE-us)

Age: 200–180 mya
Size: 20 ft long
Weight: Unknown
Location: China
Food: Herbivore

A prosauropod that walked on its hind legs and on broad feet, Lufengosaurus had knife-like teeth spaced wide apart for tearing up tough vegetation. Its teeth also give the indication that Lufengosaurus may have eaten some small animals. A huge claw topped each thumb, and its fingers were long. Lufengosaurus had several bony lumps around its jaw and on its snout. Scientists named Lufengosaurus the "Lu-Feng lizard" after the area where they found its remains.

Magnosaurus (MAG-no-SORE-us)

Age: 175 mya
Size: 13 ft
Weight: 1,100 lbs
Location: England: Dorset
Food: Carnivore

Originally identified as a Megalosaurus, this dinosaur received its own genus in 1932 as Friedrich von Huene correctly reclassified it. The bones so closely resembled Megalosaurus that von Huene gave it a name that also means "great lizard." After von Huene's time, the bones lay in storage without additional study until Roger Benson, a Cambridge University paleontologist, took an interest in them in 2010. He made a detailed study of the remains and finally confirmed Magnosaurus as a separate dinosaur with a jawbone that had features completely different from other dinosaurs.

Mamenchisaurus (ma-MEN-chee-SORE-us)

Age: 160–145 mya
Size: 82 ft long
Weight: 35.4 tons
Location: China
Food: Herbivore

Mamenchisaurus had one of the longest necks of any of the sauropods. Some specimens had necks 31 to 36 feet long. Its neck made up well more than half of its total body length. Perched atop this incredibly large neck was a tiny head, just 2 feet long. The 19 vertebrae—the most of any known dinosaur—were hollow in order to lighten the neck enough that Mamenchisaurus could lift it.

This was another dinosaur that sparked a debate among scientists as to whether Mamenchisaurus lifted its head to reach tall treetops, or simply moved its head side-to-side at ground level, consuming vegetation like a vacuum cleaner. Very high blood pressure and a massive heart would be needed to send blood flowing upward when its head was lifted to the full extent of its neck. Mamenchisaurus's name means "Mamen Brook lizard," after the Chinese village where fossil hunters discovered its remains.

Marshosaurus (MARSH-oh-SORE-us)

Age: 154–142 mya
Size: 16 ft long
Weight: 440 lbs
Location: USA: Colorado, Utah
Food: Carnivore

Curved teeth with serrated edges mounted in a jaw that was 2 feet long made Marshosaurus a ferocious predator. The dinosaur was named for Othniel C. Marsh, an early fossil hunter, in 1976 because Marshosaurus's bones were uncovered in the Cleveland-Lloyd Quarry, a location frequented by Marsh. When discovered, Marshosaurus bones were among several Allosaurus remains, suggesting these two dinosaurs may have lived in harmony with each other.

Massospondylus (MASS-oh-SPON-dih-lus)

Age: 198–188 mya

Size: 13 ft long

Weight: 300 lbs

Location: USA: Arizona; Lesotho; South Africa; Zimbabwe

Food: Herbivore

This prosauropod's name means "massive vertebrae" for its spinal bones. Originally named by Sir Richard Owen in 1854, Massospondylus fossils have since been found in several locations in Africa. In 1985, a Massospondylus skull was uncovered in Arizona, showing that the dinosaur lived in two opposite areas when the world's large land masses were still connected to one another.

Massospondylus's upper jaw jutted out a bit. Its hands had five fingers, which Massospondylus used to grip and hold tree branches while it stripped them of leaves. It also had long claws on its thumbs, which may have aided in ripping plants to bite-sized pieces.

Excavations beginning in 2006 exposed a large number of Massospondylus eggs near what was a lake in the Jurassic Period. The eggs were stacked in layers, suggesting that Massospondylus used the same nesting site more than once. While an adult Massospondylus walked on two legs, young hatchlings appear to have walked on all fours because their legs were all the same length.

Megalosaurus (MEG-ah-lo-SORE-us)

Age: 166 mya
Size: 30 ft long
Weight: 1.9 tons
Location: England, France
Food: Carnivore

Long, sharp claws and fearsome curved teeth earned this dinosaur its name, which means "great lizard." Megalosaurus was the first dinosaur ever identified after its jaw was discovered in an English quarry in 1815. Oxford University's first geology professor, William Buckland, named it in 1824. Dinosaurs were not very well understood at the time, and it was not until 1842 that Sir Richard Owen attributed the remains to those of a dinosaur. Over the years, scientists applied the Megalosaurus name to many other dinosaur finds. Most of them ended up being the bones of entirely different species.

Megalosaurus was another Jurassic Period killer. It walked on two legs, attacking its prey with incredible speed. A muscular frame, strong arms, clawed fingers and knife-like teeth made Megalosaurus a feared predator.

Drawing of the right lower jaw from William Buckland's "Notice on the Megalosaurus or great Fossil Lizard of Stonesfield." 1824.

Megapnosaurus (meg-APP-no-sore-us)

Age: 199–198 mya

Size: 10 ft long

Weight: 70 lbs

Location: Zimbabwe; Southwestern USA

Food: Carnivore

Paleontologists digging at a site in Zimbabwe in the 1960s uncovered around 30 skeletons grouped together. This suggested that Megapnosaurus may have been a pack hunter. The fossilized bones and impressions indicated that Megapnosaurus was lean, quick, and may have sported feathers.

Mike Raath named the dinosaur "Syntarsus," but 30 years later, entomologists discovered that a beetle already had that name. The entomologists called the dinosaur Megapnosaurus, which means "big dead lizard," a joke that paleontologists did not find funny. Not only were the entomologists poking fun at the science of studying dinosaurs, but the description was not accurate, as Megapnosaurus was only a modestly sized animal. However, rules dictate that, after the announcement of the new name, it has to be used.

Metriacanthosaurus (MET-ree-ah-CANTH-oh-SORE-us)

Age: 160 mya

Size: 26 ft long

Weight: 1,980 lbs

Location: England

Food: Carnivore

Fossil collector James Parker found the scattered and broken remains of Metriacanthosaurus in the 1800s. Because a skull was not among the fragments, little is known about how Metriacanthosaurus in relates to other dinosaurs of the time. A small ridge along the spine leant this dinosaur its name, which means "moderately spined lizard."

Miragaia (MIR-ah-GUY-ah)

Age: 150–143 mya
Size: 20 ft long
Weight: 1.9 tons
Location: Portugal
Food: Herbivore

A partial skeleton described in 2009 revealed that Miragaia had a longer neck than most of its stegosaur cousins. Instead of the typical 12 to 15 vertebrae, Miragaia had at least 17. This dinosaur had bony plates similar to those of Stegosaurus, except that they were smaller. Miragaia also had spikes for defense.

Monolophosaurus (MON-oh-LOAF-oh-SORE-us)

Age: 170 mya
Size: 20 ft
Weight: 1,500 lbs
Location: China
Food: Carnivore

A long, bony ridge that extended from Monolophosaurus's nose to the top of its head gave rise to its name, which means "single crested lizard." The crest was hollow, which may have created a chamber from which Monolophosaurus could have made loud sounds. This species also had large nostrils, and its lower jaw was slender. One of the first of the large carnivores.

Mymoorapelta (my-MOOR-ah-PELT-ah)

Age: 155–145 mya
Size: 10 ft long
Weight: 660 lbs
Location: USA: Colorado
Food: Herbivore

An armored plant eater, Mymoorapelta was one of the early ankylosaurs. It stood close to the ground, foraging for low growing plants. Described in 1994, Mymoorapelta had sharp spikes along its sides, tough and thick scutes (plates) on its back, and a dense skull. All of these features made it difficult for theropod predators to successfully attack the well-armed Mymoorapelta. The remains came from the Mygatt-Moore Quarry, from which this dinosaur got its name.

Ornitholestes (ORN-ith-oh-LEST-ease)

Age: 154 mya
Size: 6 ft
Weight: 24 lbs
Location: USA: Wyoming
Food: Carnivore

This light, swift, and rather small predator probably darted about in Jurassic woodlands. It was an impressive hunter that had both cone-shaped teeth and smaller, curved teeth. All that is known about Ornitholestes comes from a single skeleton found in 1900 and named "bird robber" by American paleontologist Henry Fairfield Osborn. Birds may have been part of its diet, but it probably ate whatever it could catch, including small mammals, lizards, reptiles, and baby dinosaurs.

Ornitholestes had a tail that made up more than half of its length. It had long arms, and fingers tipped with sharp claws. The partial skeleton made scientists wonder if Ornitholestes also had a small crest near its nostrils.

Mary Anning

History has had many excellent fossil hunters and paleontologists. None may have been as little honored yet as deserving of recognition than Mary Anning (1799–1847).

While strolling a beach in England with her brother when she was 11, the pair happened on a large, fossilized head. She was hooked, and became a famous fossil hunter. She spent many months uncovering her first find, later named Ichthyosaurus, the "fish lizard."

As a poor woman with little education, the scientific community scoffed at Anning. At the time, only wealthy men were considered respected scientists. That did not stop Anning. She taught herself everything she could about the fossils she continued finding. Her notes were detailed and her sketches carefully drawn with accuracy.

One geologist, Henry De la Beche, believed in Anning and her work. In 1830, he painted a watercolor using her notes and sketches. He hoped to sell prints in order to raise money to help Anning. His painting, Duria Antiquior, showed an accurate picture of prehistoric life. And it contained dozens of specimens, all of them discovered by Anning.

Ozraptor (OZ-rap-tore)

Age: 170 mya
Size: 6.5 ft
Weight: 100 lbs
Location: Western Australia
Food: Carnivore

In the mid-1960s, four schoolboys found a bone sticking out of some rocks near the town of Geraldton. The boys called the University of Western Australia to report what they saw. The university took a cast of the bone and sent it to the Natural History Museum in London, which reported the find as a turtle bone.

Thirty years later, paleontologists finally chipped away at the rock and freed the bone, a 3-inch-long piece of a shinbone. Further research revealed the bone fragment came from a theropod with an ankle joint that indicated a speedy predator, later named Ozraptor, that hunted in Australia's Jurassic woodlands.

Poekilopleuron (POE-kill-oh-PLURE-on)

Age: 170–165 mya
Size: 30 ft long
Weight: 1,800 lbs
Location: France: Normandy
Food: Carnivore

Unlike later theropods, such as Tyrannosaurus, Poekilopleuron's arms were not scrawny at all. They were muscular, powerful, and very likely were this predator's biggest weapon as it hunted other dinosaurs. Heavy for its size, Poekilopleuron was probably very slow, so it could not chase its prey. The name means "varied ribs" because three very different types of bones made up Poekilopleuron's complete fossilized ribcage.

Proceratosaurus (PRO-say-RAT-oh-SORE-us)

Age: 165 mya
Size: 10 ft long
Weight: 110 lbs
Location: England
Food: Carnivore

An almost complete skull discovered in 1910 is all that was found of Proceratosaurus. The skull's shape and size make scientists think that Proceratosaurus was an early relative of the tyrannosaurs. A strange-looking crest on the tip of the snout is different from other similar dinosaur skulls. Scientists cannot be certain that the crest is not part of a larger structure because the top of the skull was not preserved. Proceratosaurus was related to Ceratosaurus, and its name means "before Ceratosaurus."

Jurassic

Rhoetosaurus (row-toe-SORE-us)

Age: 150–180 mya

Size: 48 ft long

Weight: 15 tons

Location: Australia

Food: Herbivore

Rhoetosaurus was the first large sauropod found in Australia. It lived in what was then a lush, fertile land with tall trees and plenty of vegetation. Originally, only a few tail vertebrae and part of a hip were found. Later, a pelvis, leg bone, and rib fragments were uncovered. Rhoetosaurus was a typical sauropod with a long neck and tail and a massive body. Heber Longman first described Rhoetosaurus, and he named it in 1926. The name means "Rhoetos lizard." Rhoetos is a character in Greek mythology.

Saurophaganax (SORE-oh-FAG-ah-nax)

Age: 150–145 mya

Size: 42 ft long

Weight: 5 tons

Location: USA: Oklahoma, New Mexico

Food: Carnivore

Close to the size of a Tyrannosaurus, Saurophaganax looked like a beefed up version of Allosaurus. Some paleontologists suggest it may even have been a type of Allosaurus. Its large, intimidating size gave rise to its name, which means "king of the lizard eaters."

The first remains, a partial skeleton, emerged from an Oklahoma ranch in 1931, and made Saurophaganax Oklahoma's official state fossil. A larger specimen found in New Mexico is still under study.

Jurassic

Scelidosaurus (SKELL-ih-doe-SORE-us)

Age: 200 mya

Size: 13 ft long

Weight: 500 lbs

Location: USA: Arizona; England; Tibet

Food: Herbivore

Scelidosaurus walked slowly on all fours, low to the ground, consuming short-growing vegetation. Its body was armored and heavy, its head small. Scelidosaurus had a longer neck than most other armored dinosaurs. Its neck, back, and tail were protected by rows of bony plates. Because it could not move very quickly, its defense may have been to hug the ground and hope its thick armor was tough enough to deter any theropods that tried attacking it.

Scelidosaurus's name means "limb lizard." All the fossils found of this dinosaur came from rocks that had been in an ancient sea floor. As a result, some paleontologists believe that Scelidosaurus was amphibious. However, it is likely more probable that it lived along riverbanks, and may have drowned after being washed in or slipping.

Sciurumimus (SIGH-oor-uh-MEE-mus)

Age: 150 mya

Size: 20 ft long

Weight: 1 ton

Location: Germany

Food: Carnivore

In 2012, scientists found a juvenile specimen barely more than 2 feet long. Its adult size and weight are estimates. Sciurumimus's fossilized remains gave clear evidence of a bushy squirrel-like tail as well as fuzzy feathers in patches along its body. Its tail gives it its name, which means "squirrel mimic." Sciurumimus's dinosaur fuzz was a surprise to paleontologists because it appeared earlier and in a different group of dinosaurs than previously found.

Scutellosaurus (SKOO-tell-oh-SORE-us)

Age: 196 mya
Size: 4 ft long
Weight: 20 lbs
Location: USA: Arizona
Food: Herbivore

The "little shield lizard" had more than 300 short, bony spikes covering its back, sides, and tail. It also had a row or two of scutes on its back. While this armor provided Scutellosaurus with a protective shield, it made the beast heavy for its small size. Even so, Scutellosaurus had strong legs that allowed it to move quickly. It could choose to run from danger, or drop to the ground in hopes that a predator's teeth could not get past the bony plates and spikes.

Segisaurus (say-ee-SORE-us)

Age: 200 mya
Size: 3 ft long
Weight: 11 lbs
Location: USA: Arizona
Food: Carnivore

Although very small, the few bones discovered suggest that Segisaurus was a theropod. It was likely a swift runner that could dart and weave as it pursued its prey. The name means "Segi lizard" after the area in which its fossils were found.

Seitaad (SAY-todd)

Age: 185 mya
Size: 15 ft long
Weight: 200 lbs
Location: USA: Utah
Food: Herbivore

Navajo Indian tales describe a monster named Seit'aad that buried its victims in the sand dunes of the southwest. Seitaad takes its name from this legend as its remains were encased in a Navajo sandstone formation. In the Jurassic Period, the part of Utah in which Seitaad lived was a large desert. The skull and tail had long since withered to dust, but scientists found some limbs and a torso. Seitaad's body was curled unnaturally as if a sudden sandstorm had entombed it.

Did Dinosaurs Communicate?

Many scientists agree that dinosaurs were able to produce sounds. No one knows for certain because the soft tissues used to create sounds do not fossilize well. Birds and some reptiles, which are close relatives of the dinosaurs, make sounds to attract mates, warn of danger, or indicate that they are hurt. Dinosaurs had structures that allowed them to hear sounds, so it seems logical they must have produced them, too. Some hadrosaurs, such as Lambeosaurus, had crests with convoluted air chambers that many paleontologists think were used for amplifying sounds. These chambers may have helped Lambeosaurus make loud trumpeting noises to keep track of its herd.

Shunosaurus (SHOE-no-SORE-us)

Age: 165–161 mya
Size: 31 ft long
Weight: 2.9 tons
Location: Central China
Food: Herbivore

Shunosaurus fossils first emerged in 1977, but they were not examined in detail by paleontologists for more than a decade. A nearly complete skeleton showed that Shunosaurus's defensive characteristics included a spiked tail that it could swing at enemies trying to attack it. Although smaller than most sauropods, Shunosaurus had their familiar features: massive body size, a long tail, and a long neck. Scientists found Shunosaurus's skeleton in a Chinese province called Sichuan. The name means "Shu lizard." Shu is the ancient name for the Sichuan province.

Sinraptor (SIN-rap-tore)

Age: 168–156 mya
Size: 25 ft.
Weight: 1.3 tons
Location: China
Food: Carnivore

A smaller theropod, Sinraptor was likely still near the top of the food chain in the area in which it lived. Its name means "Chinese thief." Sinraptor may have engaged in terrible fights with other Sinraptors and possibly even fed on others of its kind. This is evidenced by Sinraptor tooth marks on some specimens.

Velociraptors, from the Cretaceous Period

Jurassic

65

Spinophorosaurus (SPY-no-FOR-oh-SORE-us)

Age: 170–165 mya
Size: 43 ft long
Weight: 6.8 tons
Location: Niger
Food: Herbivore

This sauropod's remains emerged in 2009 as an almost complete and well-preserved skeleton. Its spiked tail was even larger and more ferocious than the one that armed Shunosaurus. Two pairs of sharp spikes on the end of a long tail provided a dangerous means of self-defense. The spikes on both Spinophorosaurus and Shunosaurus were very similar to the ones that Stegosaurus had. In celebration of the spikes, Spinophorosaurus's name means "spine bearing lizard."

How Old Are Those Bones?

Scientists use several different methods to accurately date the age of fossils. One method compares the age of the fossil to the age of surrounding rock. Another measures the age of the fossil using an accurate clock, but not the kind of clock that we use in homes. A third method measures the direction in which magnetic rocks point.

Stegosaurus (steg-oh-SORE-us)

Age: 150 mya
Size: 30 ft long
Weight: 2.2 tons
Location: USA: Colorado, Utah, Wyoming; Portugal
Food: Herbivore

Stegosaurus is the largest known specimen of the plated dinosaurs. Its features included plates that rose upward from the neck, back and the upper portion of its tail. These plates did not appear effective as defense armor and scientists speculate they may have helped Stegosaurus heat and cool its body. At its hips, Stegosaurus stood 8 feet tall, about the distance from the floor to the ceiling of a typical house. Stegosaurus had two pairs of spikes on its tail. It could swing these at predators, or back into its enemies like a porcupine. Scientists call Stegosaurus's spikes (as well as those on other dinosaurs) thagomizers. This was a made up term used by cartoonist Gary Larson, but it stuck.

When Othniel C. Marsh first discovered a Stegosaurus fossil, he thought he had found a huge turtle. He thought that the large, bony plates covering the fossil's back looked like roof tiles. Once he found the skull, he knew he had discovered a new kind of dinosaur. He gave it a name meaning "roof lizard" for his initial impression of what the animal looked like. In 1992, paleontologists discovered more bony plates over Stegosaurus's hips, plus some bony studs around its neck.

Supersaurus (SOO-per-SORE-us)

Age: 153 mya
Size: 112 ft long
Weight: 34.4 tons
Location: USA: Colorado
Food: Herbivore

At 49 feet from shoulders to skull, Supersaurus had the longest neck of any dinosaur yet discovered. Its complete skeleton was among a heap of fossilized bones found in Colorado. Some scientists speculate that a large number of sauropods may have died during a drought period before a flash flood pushed the bones to the location where they were discovered. A cast of the complete Supersaurus skeleton is on display at the Wyoming Dinosaur Center.

Although it was not the largest, heaviest dinosaur ever found, Supersaurus's name means "super lizard," referring to its long neck. Much debate circulates among paleontologists about why sauropods developed such long necks. Theories include the ability to reach taller treetops, sweeping across low vegetation like a vacuum cleaner, and pushing deep into thick forests where its body could not follow.

Szechuanosaurus (sue-CHWAN-oh-SORE-us)

Age: 156–145 mya
Size: 20 ft long
Weight: 300 lbs
Location: China
Food: Carnivore

Szechuanosaurus resembled an Allosaurus, but was much smaller. It looked fierce, with strong legs and a huge head filled with curved, pointed teeth. Szechuanosaurus also had a short neck and arms, but each of its three-fingered hands were clawed for ripping and tearing. Chinese paleontologist Chung Chien Young found Szechuanosaurus in 1942, and he named it for the province where he discovered its remains.

Jurassic

Tianchisaurus (TYAN-chee-SORE-us)

Age: 170–168 mya

Size: 10 ft long

Weight: 660 lbs

Location: China: Sangonghe Valley

Food: Herbivore

Tianchisaurus was the first known ankylosaur, the heavily armored herbivores. It had a layer of thick armor covering its back and a small club at the end of its tail. The club could be swung at enemies as a means of defense. A group of geology students found Tianchisaurus's bones in 1974. Originally named Jurassosaurus, the dinosaur was renamed "heavenly lake lizard" by palenotolgist Dong Zhiming to describe where the fossils were uncovered.

Tianchisaurus was originally named Jurassosaurus in honor of the movie *Jurassic Park*, because its director, Steven Spielberg, helped fund the dig. Although the genus name changed, the odd sounding species name—nedegoapeferima—is made from fragments of the last names of *Jurassic Park* movie stars: Sam Neil, Laura Dern, Jeff Goldblum, Richard Attenborough, Bob Peck, Martin Ferrero, Ariana Richards, and Joseph Mazzello.

Torvosaurus (TORE-voh-SORE-us)

Age: 153–148 mya
Size: 30 ft long
Weight: 1.9 tons
Location: USA: Colorado; Portugal
Food: Carnivore

The only confirmed fossil belonging to Torvosaurus was a section of one of its forelimbs. Since then, fossil hunters discovered other bone fragments including pieces of a jawbone, a partial hip, some vertebrae, and a skull section. Enough bone fragments demonstrate that Torvosaurus was probably the largest carnivore of its day. It had small arms, but they were strong, and it bore large claws on its hands. These features gave Torvosaurus its name, meaning "savage lizard."

Tuojiangosaurus (TOO-YANG-oh-SORE-us)

Age: 160 mya
Size: 23 ft long
Weight: 3.9 tons
Location: China
Food: Herbivore

The "Tuo River lizard" had a bulky, arched body, a small head with a toothless beak, and a stout tail. The tip of the tail bore two pairs of bony spikes. In addition, Tuojiangosaurus had 15 pairs of bony plates along its back. Each plate rose to points. This Stegosaurus relative was well equipped to defend itself. Paleontologists described Tuojiangosaurus from two well-preserved skeletons found near the Tuo River in China. Built low to the ground, Tuojiangosaurus ambled along ancient riverbanks, consuming all of the low-growing vegetation it could eat. Small cheek teeth ground the plant material as it chewed.

Turiasaurus (TOOR-ee-ah-SORE-us)

Age: 145 mya
Size: 98 ft long
Weight: 49 tons
Location: Eastern Spain
Food: Herbivore

The largest land animal ever to have lived in Europe, Turiasaurus was also the first large sauropod found on that continent. Its vertebrae indicate that it may have had a row of spikes along its backbone. Turiasaurus ate whatever plant material it could reach, grinding the vegetation with the help of heart-shaped teeth coated with wavy enamel. Turiasaurus means "Turia lizard," a name that refers to the Latin word for the province in which its fossils emerged.

Veterupristisaurus (VET-er-oo-PRIST-ee-SORE-us)

Age: 154–150 mya
Size: 33 ft long
Weight: 2.9 tons
Location: Tanzania
Food: Carnivore

German paleontologist Oliver Rauhut saw enough from just the few vertebrae found to declare in 2011 that Veterupristisaurus belonged to a family of dinosaurs that had huge jaws similar to those of modern sharks. The Cretaceous Period's Giganotosaurus was also a member of this family. Because Veterupristisaurus came along earlier, Rauhut gave it a name meaning "old shark lizard." He also used the vertebrae to estimate this predator's size and weight.

Vulcanodon (vul-CAN-oh-don)

Age: 208–201 mya
Size: 21 ft long
Weight: 2.5 tons
Location: Zimbabwe
Food: Herbivore

Because it was found between what were two Jurassic lava beds, Vulcanodon earned the name "volcano tooth." It was a very early sauropod that walked on short, stubby legs. Like other sauropods, it probably plodded along, as its pillar-like legs were suited to support huge weight, but were not built for running.

Xiaotingia (zhow-TIN-gee-ah)

Age: 165–153 mya
Size: 2 ft long
Weight: 5 lbs
Location: China: Liaoning
Food: Insectivore, possibly an omnivore

At first, its feathers and a long tail categorized Xiaotingia as a bird. A more thorough examination of its bones revealed that it actually belonged in a family of theropods called troodontids. These dinosaurs had several characteristics in common with birds, but were only bird-like. Xiaotingia, named in honor of a natural history museum founder, probably fed on insects. However, the shape of its teeth suggests that it may have also preyed on shellfish and consumed plants.

Yangchuanosaurus (yan-WHO-an-owe-SORE-us)

Age: 150 mya
Size: 30 ft long
Weight: 2 tons
Location: China
Food: Carnivore

A dam builder in China made the first discovery of Yangchuanosaurus bones in 1978. A few years later, a second set of bones emerged from the same rock formation. Yangchuanosaurus is named for the region in which it was found. Short arms, sharp claws, a powerful jaw full of sharp teeth and strong legs make Yangchuanosaurus very similar in appearance to Allosaurus. It also had ridges down its back and a knob protruding from its snout.

Yizhousaurus (YEE-zoo-SORE-us)

Age: 199–196 mya
Size: 33 ft long
Weight: Unknown
Location: Southern China
Food: Herbivore

Scientists have continued studying Yizhousaurus long after its complete skeleton emerged in 2005. This dinosaur fits a missing link between prosauropods and sauropods. The intact skull in particular shows the features paleontologists expect from a large herbivore. Although much smaller than the great beasts to come, Yizhousaurus walked about on four legs instead of two, and its neck and tail were longer than its prosauropod cousins.

Yunnanosaurus (you-NAN-oh-SORE-us)

Age: 200–185 mya
Size: 23 ft long
Weight: 1,500 lbs
Location: Southern China
Food: Herbivore

Yunnanosaurus was a rich find in the Yunnan Province of China, an area from which this dinosaur gets its name. Scientists uncovered 20 skeletons, two of which included skulls. One of those skulls contained 60 teeth. The shape of the teeth shows a dinosaur that spent its time chewing plant material in Jurassic woodlands. An examination of wear patterns on the teeth suggest that Yunnanosaurus kept them sharp by grinding them together as it chewed.

Dino Droppings

Add something to the list of dinosaur remnants found by paleontologists and fossil hunters: coprolites, or dinosaur dung. Studying dinosaur poop may not seem like someone's dream job, but it does provide a great deal of evidence about what dinosaurs ate.

Once mined in England as fertilizer because they were rich in phosphorus, coprolites were finally recognized for what they really were during the 1830s. Famous fossil hunter Mary Anning found stones in dinosaur bellies and said she found fish bones inside those stones. William Buckland named them with a Greek term that means "dung stones."

Karen Chin has a large collection of coprolites, and she is recognized as a world expert in dino dung. She slices them into thin sections and looks at them under a microscope. She searches for seeds, scales, bones, and leaves. She has even uncovered evidence that dung beetles were hard at work doing their thankless task during the age of the dinosaurs.

DIGGING DEEPER

Dinosaurs and Birds: Are They Related?

Look outside your window. It probably will not take long to see birds pecking at seeds and insects on the ground or flying by in the distance. Are you looking at dinosaurs? Most paleontologists would say you are.

A few scientists argue differently, but the largest group agree that modern birds evolved from the lizard-hipped theropods that included the great carnivores, such as Allosaurus, Velociraptor, and Tyrannosaurus. That may seem a little odd because the other large family of dinosaurs were bird-hipped, but the similarities between the features and behavior of theropods and modern birds is striking.

Paleontologists studying theropods are finding more and more of them had feathers, or at least a fluffy down. They had yet to develop flight muscles, but those may have still been evolving. As you read some of the descriptions of dinosaurs in this book, you will discover that many had wrist and joint bones that closely resembled those found in birds. Hollow bones for weight reduction were also developing in many dinosaurs, as was a wishbone, just like those found in birds. Some dinosaur parents, such as Velociraptor, took turns brooding over the eggs laid in neat nests.

In 2007, two important discoveries went even further toward making the connection between dinosaurs and birds.

The first was by Mary Higby Schweitzer. She and her team discovered blood vessels and even blood cells in the leg bone of a Tyrannosaurus and analyzed them. Their structure matched those of today's emus and ostriches. The study brought plenty of controversy as some scientists argued that soft tissues like blood vessels would never make it through fossilization. They thought the tissues may have come from something else. Schweitzer and her team suggest that iron helped preserve the tender tissues.

The second discovery also came from Schweitzer's tissue discovery. John Asara, of Harvard Medical School, compared the protein from the blood sample against those of modern-day animals. He found that the closest match was to the protein of a chicken. Could the mighty Tyrannosaurus rex be an ancestor of the main ingredient in chicken noodle soup?

Although a mass extinction at the end of the Cretaceous Period wiped out well more than half the life on Earth, we know that some species managed to survive. The huge dinosaurs were gone, so was most anything else larger than a dog. But birds that had evolved into smaller sizes made it. And if those birds were dinosaurs, then the smallest dinosaurs survived.

Take a closer look at that wishbone from the holiday turkey. You are examining a key piece of structure that links together the birds of today with the incredible dinosaurs from millions of years ago.

Tracking Dinosaurs

Although it may seem impossible to find dinosaur tracks after millions of years, their footprints are present in hundreds of areas all over the world. Muddy banks along streams, ponds, lakes, and seas provided an area for dinosaurs to leave tracks as they stopped to fish or get a drink. Once the mud dried, sediment or soils may have filled the tracks and, over long periods of time, the sediment and the material around the tracks hardened into stone. Erosion eventually brought the tracks back to the surface.

Tracks are a wonderful find for paleontologists. They provide a means of estimating the weight of dinosaurs, a hint of the way species walked, demonstrate the speed at which dinosaurs moved, and determine whether individuals dragged their tails or held them above the ground.

Tracks may be found in Alaska, Arkansas, Colorado, Connecticut, Wyoming, and many other states mostly in the south or west. Canada and Scotland also have sites of well-preserved dinosaur tracks.

Triceratops

Stegosaurus

Tyrannosaurus Rex

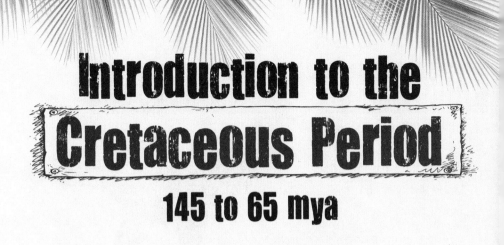

Introduction to the Cretaceous Period

145 to 65 mya

Dinosaurs became the masters of the Earth during the Jurassic Period, and their reign continued through the Cretaceous Period. No great extinction occurred as the Cretaceous Period began. Instead, dinosaurs became more diverse and specialized as the period moved forward.

The massive and fearsome predator, Tyrannosaurus, emerged with a combination of intelligence and power. Some herbivores developed thick armor plating as a way to combat the lethal bite of strong predators. Huge seemed to be the order of the day as the massive beasts of the Jurassic grew taller, longer, wider, and stronger.

Gondwana split into some of the southern continents we might recognize. Laurasia would not do so until almost the end of the period. The drift in continents led to dinosaurs developing differently in different parts of the world. A shallow ocean cut through the middle of what would someday become North America. Mud beds turned to rock over the period, which formed Niobrara chalk, a rich source of fossils and the Latin word for which the Cretaceous Period earned its name.

Familiar tree species, such as oaks, walnuts, and maples evolved. The world began to get more color as flowers dotted the landscape. Early flowering plants included magnolias and passionflowers. Where flowers form, fruits follow and the Cretaceous Period saw the first of them. Flowers also brought the emergence of pollinators such as bees and beetles.

Mammals began rising up from the tiny mouse-like creatures and birds started to take wing. Oceans were filled with fish and reptile predators. The skies saw larger and stronger pterosaurs.

Then it all came to a stop. A mass extinction wiped out the huge dinosaurs for good. They would never return, at least not in that form. But their descendants survived, and they survive to this day. Other organisms also survived, including insects, jellyfish, and others. And the rise of mammals was just around the next bend.

Albertosaurus (al-BERT-oh-SORE-us)

Age: 75 mya
Size: 30 ft long
Weight: 3 tons
Location: Canada
Food: Carnivore

Albertosaurus was a large predator related to Tyrannosaurus, but arriving several million years earlier. It looked much like T. rex, but it was lighter, indicating it could move swiftly when chasing prey. Albertosaurus also had a long tail that aided its balance and helped it make quick turns. A massive head had two small horns near the eyes. Its jaws were lined with banana-shaped teeth designed for crunching through bones and tearing chunks of flesh. Albertosaurus was named for Alberta, Canada, the location of the first find.

Amargasaurus (ah-MAR-gah-SORE-us)

Age: 130–120 mya
Size: 36 ft long
Weight: 3.9 tons
Location: Argentina
Food: Herbivore

Discovered in the La Amarga Canyon in 1984, the single skeleton showed one very unusual feature: a double row of long spikes down Amargasaurus' neck and back. Some paleontologists argue that the spikes were covered with skin to form a sail. Others counter that the bony spikes were coated in horn material and rattled to make a loud noise.

Ankylosaurus (ANK-ill-oh-SORE-us)

Age: 70–65 mya

Size: 23 ft long

Weight: 2.9 tons

Location: USA: Montana, Wyoming; Canada: Alberta

Food: Herbivore

Ankylosaurus means "bent lizard," and it also lent its name to a whole group of armored dinosaurs called ankylosaurs. This species was the largest of the group. Ankylosaurus was a plodding animal that grazed on low-growing vegetation. It did not have a large brain, and it could not move quickly to escape danger. Its defense was the presence of hundreds of studded armored plates across its thick skin. Ankylosaurus's eyelids were even covered with plates. These plates were bony and they grew from the skin, much like the plates on a crocodile. As well as all that armor, Ankylosaurus had a thick, heavy tail with a club at the end. It could swing its tail and crush the bones of predators attacking it.

Appalachiosaurus (APP-ah-LAY-sha-SORE-us)

Age: 77 mya

Size: 23 ft long

Weight: 1,980 lbs

Location: USA: Alabama

Food: Carnivore

During the Cretaceous Period, an island was just east of the shallow sea that cut through the heart of the North American continent. Part of that island included what is now Alabama, where Appalachiosaurus, named after the Appalachian Mountains, was found. It was the largest theropod from the eastern states, and it had yet to reach adulthood. It lived about 7 million years earlier than other tyrannosaurs.

Argentinosaurus (ARE-jen-teen-oh-SORE-us)

Age: 96–94 mya
Size: 98 ft long
Weight: 74 tons
Location: Argentina
Food: Herbivore

In 1988, an Argentine farmer named Guillermo Heredia found what he thought was a large piece of wood on his land. Paleontologists realized it was a 5-foot section of shinbone. As they dug, they found more huge bones, including a 6-foot-tall vertebra. The skeletons were far from complete, but there were enough critical bones that scientists estimated Argentinosaurus's size and weight. They discovered that this was among the largest, if not the largest, land animal to have ever walked the Earth. It was nearly 100 feet long and weighed as much as 14 elephants. Standing with its neck stretched, it could reach as high as a 7-story building.

Avimimus (av-ih-MIME-us)

Age: 83 mya
Size: 5 ft long
Weight: 33 lbs
Location: Mongolia
Food: Omnivore

Named the "bird mimic" because it had many characteristics in common with birds. Avimimus had long legs, a very light build, and a toothless beak. Its neck was curved and its head short. Although no feather impressions were among the fossils, Avimimus had ridges along its forearms that indicate it may have had feathers. These were likely more for warmth than flight. Russian paleontologist Sergei Kurzanov discovered Avimimus and named the dinosaur in 1981.

Bambiraptor (BAM-bee-RAP-tore)

Age: 75 mya

Size: 2 ft long

Weight: 7 lbs

Location: USA: Montana

Food: Carnivore

Wes Linster, a 14-year-old boy, was fossil hunting in Glacier National Park with his parents in 1995. He discovered what turned out to be an almost perfect skeleton of a small, fast, meat-eating dinosaur. Scientists studying the find named it in honor of Bambi, the Disney cartoon character. Bambiraptor was birdlike in appearance and likely bore feathers. The shape and size of its hind legs suggest it ran quickly, and a large brain compared to its body size might indicate high intelligence.

Baryonyx (bah-ree-ON-ix)

Age: 120 mya

Size: 30 ft long

Weight: 1.1 tons

Location: England, Spain, Niger

Food: Carnivore

William Walker, a plumber and avid fossil hunter, discovered the first Baryonyx claw in a layer of clay. He called paleontologists at London's Natural History Museum. Eventually, scientists there uncovered almost 70% of a Baryonyx skeleton. The skull was nearly perfect, with a crocodile-like jaw containing 96 sharp, pointed teeth. The snout had a small crest. Huge thumb claws—12 inches long—were perfect for nabbing fish, and probably for defense. Fish scales and bones in its stomach region give further evidence of Baryonyx's diet.

Borogovia (BORE-oh-GO-vee-ah)

Age: 70–65 mya
Size: 6.5 ft long
Weight: 25 lbs
Location: Mongolia
Food: Carnivore

Many people recall Lewis Carroll's poem, "Jabberwocky," with its twisting tale of gibberish words and odd creatures. In it, he mentions the "borogoves," which Alice later learns in *Through the Looking Glass* is "a thin shabby-looking bird with its feathers sticking out all round." Polish paleontologist Halszka Osmólska decided that was the perfect name for her new dinosaur discovery. A bird-like hunter with a toothed beak and a long killing claw on its second toe, Borogovia ate lizards and small mammals.

Dinosaur Lifespans

Dinosaurs lived in a dangerous world. Volcanoes, floods, earthquakes, and predators all took their toll. So how long did dinosaurs live if they weren't eaten, or killed by natural events? Based on reptile growth rates and how they believed dinosaur bodies functioned, paleontologists once thought individual lifespans might be as much as 200 years. Modern techniques, however, show a much different picture. Bone developed in layers as dinosaurs aged. A cross-section of bone had rings, sort of like tree rings. Counting those rings revealed the animal's true age. Many had lifespans of 20 to about 65 years. Sue, the T. rex on display in Chicago, was about 29 when she died.

Brachylophosaurus (BRACK-ee-LOAF-oh-SORE-us)

Age: 75–65 mya
Size: 30 ft long
Weight: 3 tons
Location: USA: Montana; Canada: Alberta
Food: Herbivore

Brachylophosaurus had a spoonbill and a rectangular skull with a small, paddle-shaped crest. Male specimens seemed to have a wider crest. Very few dinosaurs emerge in a mummified condition, but a Brachylophosaurus is one such animal. Typically, only hard tissues—bones—make it through the centuries. The first Brachylophosaurus was discovered in Canada in 1936. More specimens emerged in the 1950s and in late 1988, but a 2000 find got scientists excited. It was nearly perfect and had preserved organs, muscles, tendons, and skin. Even his last meal was still preserved inside his stomach. It was a magnificent day for paleontologists.

The Brachylophosaurus found in 2000 was nicknamed "Leonardo." Only about 4 years old when he died, Leonardo's remains showed small scales up to the size of a dime covering its body, as well as a small sail frill along its back. The stomach contents were in such good shape that scientists could easily tell that Leonardo ate a meal of conifers, magnolias, and ferns before it died. Researchers also found the pollen of at least 40 different plants.

Carcharodontosaurus (CAR-ka-roe-DON-toe-SORE-us)

Age: 100–93 mya
Size: 43 ft long
Weight: 5.9 tons
Location: North Africa
Food: Carnivore

Carcharodontosaurus, or "shark-toothed lizard," was among the largest carnivores to have lived. It had a massive jaw with curved, 8-inch-long teeth. If Carcharodontosaurus could manage a single bite with those teeth, it may have been enough to tear a big enough hole in its prey to create rapid blood loss, stopping the victim quickly so that Carcharodontosaurus could finish the job.

Carnotaurus (car-nah-TORE-us)

Age: 72–69 mya
Size: 25 ft long
Weight: 1.9 tons
Location: Argentina
Food: Carnivore

A large and fearsome bipedal (walked on its hind legs), Carnotaurus was named "flesh eating bull" for the two prominent horns on its head. Its deep snout probably gave it a keen sense of smell. Carnotaurus had rows of scales along its back. Scott Persons and Phil Currie presented its most interesting feature in 2011. They had studied Carnotaurus's tailbones and concluded that the dinosaur could use its tail muscles to help work its legs when running. This would give it a power boost, maybe enabling speeds as high as 30 mph. But the tail was also very stiff, which limited Carnotaurus's ability to make quick turns.

Caudipteryx (caw-DIP-ter-ix)

Age: 120 mya
Size: 3 ft long
Weight: 5 lbs
Location: China
Food: Omnivore

Caudipteryx fossils show unmistakable tail feathers and feathers along its arms. Its arms were not long enough for flight, so Caudipteryx may have used its feathers for warmth or display. The tail feathers fanned, much like modern birds. Caudipteryx provides another clear link between dinosaurs and birds.

Centrosaurus (sen-troh-SORE-us)

Age: 75 mya
Size: 20 ft long
Weight: 1.9 tons
Location: Canada: Alberta
Food: Herbivore

Centrosaurus, the "well-horned lizard," resembled a modern-day rhino. It had a large, heavy head, hoofed toes, a small tail, and a horn at the end of its snout. Two smaller brow horns were placed one above each eye. Centrosaurus also had a rounded neck frill, and it had two more bony hooks. A jaw meant for chewing tough vegetation gave Centrosaurus a powerful bite.

Swampy forest land near winding rivers was where Centrosaurus roamed. A large dinosaur graveyard near the Canadian town of Hilda in Alberta is the final resting place of a large number of Centrosaurus dinosaurs that may have been caught in a flash flood. Paleontologists studying fossils there estimate that a herd as large as 670 individuals may have perished there.

Chasmosaurus (KAS-moe-SORE-us)

Age: 76–70 mya
Size: 26 ft long
Weight: 3.5 tons
Location: Canada: Alberta
Food: Herbivore

A rhino-like dinosaur with a huge, long neck frill, it had a short, wide horn on its snout and two smaller horns above the eyes.

Chasmosaurus's body was bulky and its head large. It had hoof-like feet on short, stout legs. The neck frill had pointed projections along its edge. It may have used the horns and projections for defense while charging enemies.

Chasmosaurus likely traveled in herds, consuming low-growing, tough vegetation. Its name means "cleft lizard."

Citipati (SIH-tee-PAH-tee)

Age: 75 mya
Size: 9 ft long
Weight: 500 lbs
Location: Mongolia
Food: Omnivore

Citipati was named "funeral pyre lord" for two murdered monks who appeared in a folklore story. Its most distinguishing characteristic was a crest on its head. Some individuals were found on nests, covering the eggs with arms that likely bore feathers. Citipati had a parrot-like beak.

Corythosaurus (ko-RITH-oh-SORE-us)

Age: 75 mya
Size: 30 ft long
Weight: 3.7 tons
Location: USA: Montana; Canada: Alberta
Food: Herbivore

Named the "helmet lizard" for the distinctive crest on its head. Male specimens had the largest crests, females were smaller, and most juveniles did not have them at all. These crests were hollowed out by twisting nasal passages. That may have allowed them to be used for making loud sounds similar to those made by a trumpet. These dinosaurs roamed the coastal plains in large herds, feeding on conifer needles, ferns, and leaves.

Deinonychus (die-NON-ee-cuss)

Age: 110 mya
Size: 11 ft long
Weight: 160 lbs
Location: USA: Montana, Oklahoma
Food: Carnivore

Named the "terrible claw" for its long, fierce claw, one on each foot. It could use this as a weapon, slashing at its victims. Capable of bringing down prey larger than itself, it is likely that Deinonychus hunted in packs. Paleontologists believe that Deinonychus was one of the more intelligent dinosaurs, and that it probably had feathers.

Dracorex (dray-CORE-ex)

Age: 66 mya

Size: 10 ft long

Weight: 99 lbs

Location: USA: South Dakota

Food: Herbivore

South Dakota was a damp forest in Dracorex time and was home to this dinosaur. Dracorex had a flat, armored skull with bumps and spiky horns. It also had a long snout and walked on its hind legs. The dino is not without controversy. Paleontologist Jack Horner takes issue with the discovery and claims that Dracorex is nothing more than a juvenile Pachycephalosaurus that has not yet grown to maturity with a fully developed skull.

Robert Bakker named Dracorex "dragon king" in 2006 because of its resemblance to mythical dragons. He added an interesting species name as well: Hogwartsia after the Hogwarts wizarding school in the Harry Potter books. So, the full name means, "dragon king of Hogwarts."

Dromaeosaurus (DROM-ee-oh-SORE-us)

Age: 75 mya
Size: 6 ft long
Weight: 33 lbs
Location: USA: Montana; Canada: Alberta
Food: Carnivore

A partial skull and other bones are all that have been found of Dromaeosaurus. It was small and light, a fast runner, and its large eyes gave it good vision. The skull is broader than that of Velociraptor, which may mean its bite was more powerful. Its name means "fast running lizard," which refers to its ability to move quickly.

Edmontonia (ED-mon-TOE-nee-ah)

Age: 74–72 mya
Size: 25 ft long
Weight: 3.9 tons
Location: USA: Montana, Texas; Canada: Alberta
Food: Herbivore

Edmontonia's body was covered in rows of scutes and spikes. It had broad horns, long and bony spikes facing forward from its sides, and a tail club. Some scientists believe the armor, and especially the spikes, were used as Edmontonia lunged toward any attackers. Tyrannosaurus would have been a formidable predator, but Edmontonia had evolved enough protective armor to ward off its attacks. Its name means "of Edmonton" for the Alberta city.

Edmontosaurus (ed-MONT-oh-SORE-us)

Age: 72–65 mya

Size: 48 ft long

Weight: 3.9 tons

Location: USA: Alaska, Colorado, Montana, North Dakota, South Dakota, Wyoming; Canada: Alberta, Saskatchewan

Food: Herbivore

The "Edmonton lizard" was a duck-billed dinosaur with powerful jaws. Its cheeks were filled with hundreds of teeth for mashing mouthfuls of vegetation. Its nasal passages included a sac that could be inflated, allowing Edmontosaurus to blast a loud, resonant call.

Because it lacked sharp teeth and claws, Edmontosaurus's best means of defense was likely to run from danger. It could move around on all fours, but probably ran on hind legs, and at speeds of up to 30 mph. One body was mummified, allowing scientists to examine its diet, which included seeds, fruit, conifer needles, and twigs.

Einiosaurus (i-nee-oh-SORE-us)

Age: 74–65 mya

Size: 15 ft long

Weight: 2 tons

Location: USA: Montana

Food: Herbivore

Einiosaurus had a neck frill with two large spikes and several smaller ones. Its most prominent feature was a large, forward-facing, curved horn on its snout. It also had bony ridges protecting the eyes. The name means "buffalo lizard," and it likely moved in herds. Scientists uncovered 15 individuals at one site. They speculate that a small herd got trapped in a mudslide or a flash flood.

Eotyrannus (EE-oh-tie-RAN-us)

Age: 130 mya
Size: 18 ft long
Weight: 500 lbs
Location: England
Food: Carnivore

A feathered ancestor of the tyrannosaurs that would appear millions of years later, its name means "dawn tyrant" in recognition of being an early relative of Tyrannosaurus. Likely a fast runner, Eotyrannus had a heavy skull, and three-fingered hands on strong forearms.

BECOMING A PALEONTOLOGIST

Paleontologists are scientists that study dinosaurs, but they are concerned with much more than that. A paleontologist studies the history of all life on Earth using fossil records as a guide. Those fossils may be from dinosaurs, but they might also be left behind by other organisms that lived in ancient times. Some paleontologists specialize in just one field, such as:

 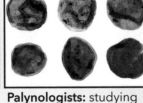 

Paleobotanists: studying the fossils of plants, fungi, or algae

Palynologists: studying fossil imprints of pollen and spores

Ichnologists: studying trails, animal tracks, and footprint impressions

Whatever fossil field you choose requires a strong background in science, especially biology and geology. Reading everything you can about dinosaurs and ancient eras is a great start. When you reach high school, take as many science classes as you can. In college, you will need to continue taking science classes and plan on getting at least a master's degree. A Ph.D. is the most common degree earned by paleontologists.

Most paleontologists work in colleges and universities where they teach classes and conduct research. Some work for museums, historical sites, or the government.

Euoplocephalus (YOU-owe-ploh-SEFF-ah-luss)

Age: 70–65 mya

Size: 23 ft long

Weight: 2 tons

Location: USA: Montana; Canada: Alberta

Food: Herbivore

Its name means "well-armored head," but Euoplocephalus was pretty well armored over its entire body. The entire top portion of its body was covered in thick plates just above its tough, leathery skin. Plus, it had rows of spikes on its body, long horns poking from the back of its head, and large spines on the sides of its head. Even Euoplocephalus's eyes were protected with bony plates. And if all that was not enough, it had a bony, club-like lump near the end of its tail that could be swung at enemies attacking it. Heavy with armor and built low to the ground, about the only way a predator could best Euoplocephalus was by flipping it over to reach the unprotected underside.

Most of the time, Euoplocephalus lumbered about on all four of its short legs. But some scientists calculated that, even for its heavy build and stocky frame, Euoplocephalus could move quickly when necessary.

Dino Eggs

Dinosaur eggs varied in size from several inches in diameter, up to about the size of a basketball. The larger the dinosaur, the bigger the egg. And the bigger the egg, the thicker the shell. If dinosaur eggs were any larger, the shells would probably be too thick for dino babies to break through.

Gallimimus (GAL-ih-MIME-us)

Age: 75–65 mya
Size: 20 ft long
Weight: 970 lbs
Location: Mongolia
Food: Omnivore

Probably the fastest sprinter of any known dinosaur, Gallimimus bolted on long legs. Its tail acted as a counter-balance for making sharp turns. Its name means "chicken mimic" because of its birdlike features. It was actually more ostrich-like in appearance, and may have run like an ostrich, too. Gallimimus had a long, thin, toothless beak and hollow bones. Its neck was also long, but its birdlike skull protected a brain that was only the size of a golf ball. It probably ate seeds, eggs, insects, and plant material.

Gastonia (gas-TOE-nee-ah)

Age: 125 mya
Size: 19 ft
Weight: 1.8 tons
Location: USA: Utah
Food: Herbivore

Robert Gaston discovered the first bones, and James Kirkland honored him when he named Gastonia in 1998. This was a very heavily armored dinosaur, covered with bumps and ridges along bony plates. It also had four rows of long, sharp spikes from its shoulders to its tail, and two rows of spikes along its tail. Gastonia lacked a clubbed tail, but it may not have been needed. The spikes could have inflicted severe injury.

Giganotosaurus (gig-AN-oh-toe-SORE-us)

Age: 97 mya
Size: 43 ft long
Weight: 7.8 tons
Location: Argentina
Food: Carnivore

Ruben Dario Carolini, an amateur fossil hunter, found the first Giganotosaurus bones in 1993. Its name means "giant southern lizard," and it may have grown even larger than Tyrannosaurus, although it lived about 30 million years before Tyrannosaurus.

Giganotosaurus hunted the vast Argentine swamps that existed during the Cretaceous Period. It had large, powerful forearms that ended in three-fingered hands. Its ferocious teeth, some as long as 8 inches, could stab victims, hold them tight, and slice through their flesh.

Gryposaurus (GRIP-oh-SORE-us)

Age: 82–74 mya
Size: 26 ft long
Weight: 2.9 tons
Location: USA: Montana; Canada: Alberta
Food: Herbivore

Named "hook-nosed lizard" for its prominent, hooked nose that made its snout look more like a beak. Its arms were long and may have been used to reach taller tree branches. Skin impressions show three different kinds of scales covering Gryposaurus's body: ones with 1.5 inch pyramids along the sides and tail, flatter scales on its sides and neck, and triangular scales running down the center of the back.

Hadrosaurus (HAD-row-SORE-us)

Age: 80–74 mya

Size: 25 ft long

Weight: 3 tons

Location: USA: New Jersey

Food: Herbivore

This duck-billed dinosaur was one of the first ever found in North America. It had a short neck, a long tail, and a bulky body. Its beak had no teeth, but it had hundreds of small teeth in its cheeks for grinding plant matter. Its back legs were much larger than its forelegs. Hadrosaurus's name means "sturdy lizard." It is the official state dinosaur of New Jersey.

Hypsilophodon (hip-sih-LO-fuh-don)

Age: 130–125 mya

Size: 7½ ft long

Weight: 45 lbs

Location: England, Spain

Food: Herbivore

Its head was small, but large eyes gave Hypsilophodon keen eyesight. It was built for speed as a means of escaping predators. Hypsilophodon lived in the swamps and coastal floodplains that were present in England during the Cretaceous Period. It had long shin bones and strong claws. Its jaws were also strong and there is evidence it may have had a cheek pouch for storing food, similar to chipmunks today. Hypsilophodon's upper teeth created a cutting edge to bite through the horsetails and ferns of its environment. That gives Hypsilophodon its name, which means "high ridge tooth."

One dig revealed several individuals clustered together, perhaps trapped in mud or quicksand.

Iguanodon (ig-WAN-oh-don)

Age: 125 mya
Size: 33 ft long
Weight: 3.1 tons
Location: Belgium, England, Germany, Spain, France
Food: Herbivore

The first Iguanodon teeth were discovered in England in 1822 either by Gideon Mantell, or his wife Mary Ann. The story changed depending on whether Gideon or someone else told it. The teeth were very similar in appearance to those belonging to iguanas, except that they were much bigger. Iguanodon earned its name for those teeth. Mantell named the dinosaur in 1825.

Hundreds of Iguanodon fossils have been uncovered since the early discovery. One large group was found in Germany, perhaps a herd caught in a flood. Iguanodon could walk on all fours, but it may have run on its hind legs. It had four fingers plus a thumb spike on each hand. The spike may have been used for defense and to tear through seed husks or fruit rinds.

Ingenia (IN-jeh-NEE-ah)

Age: 70 mya
Size: 5 ft
Weight: Unknown
Location: Mongolia
Food: Possibly an omnivore

Very few fossils have been found for this small, birdlike dinosaur. It was first discovered in the Ingen Province in Mongolia. Possibly feathered, Ingenia had bulky hands, and each hand had a large thumb along with a thumb claw.

Irritator (IH-rih-tay-tore)

Age: 110–100 mya
Size: 26 ft long
Weight: 1,800 lbs
Location: Brazil
Food: Carnivore

In 1996, a fossil hunter discovered a dinosaur skull while searching in Brazil. The hunter wanted to make the skull more valuable than he thought it was, so he disguised it as a pterosaur. As David Martill and his team began working on the skull, they realized it had an elongated nose made of plaster. That was irritating enough, but next came the difficult task of carefully removing the plaster without harming the original skull. When they discovered the skull belonged to a previously unknown dinosaur, they named it Irritator for all the grief it had brought them.

Irritator likely ate a diet of fish and maybe some small mammals. It appears to have had a sail along its back and it may have had a small crest on its head.

Hungry, Hungry Herbivores

About 70% of dinosaurs were plant eaters. The largest among them may have required as much as 100,000 calories a day to survive. By contrast, people need about 2,000 calories daily. Scientists estimate that the largest sauropods would have had to consume up to half a ton of vegetation a day! That many leaves and stems would probably fill your school bus. The Mesozoic world must have been thick with vegetation just to support dinosaur diets.

Isisaurus (Iss-ee-SORE-us)

Age: 70–65 mya
Size: 59 ft long
Weight: 14.7 tons
Location: India
Food: Herbivore

Isisaurus's neck was slender, short, and deep. Its front legs were unusually long, making its walk very much like modern hyenas. At first, scientists thought they had found a new species of Titanosaurus, but further study gave Isisaurus its own genus in 2003.

Researchers examining coprolites, or fossilized feces, from this dinosaur discovered a fungus found on many Cretaceous Era leaves. As a result, they think Isisaurus's diet included leaves from many different trees. Isisaurus was named in honor of the Indian Statistical Institute, which owns many previous fossil finds.

Lambeosaurus (LAMB-ee-oh-SORE-us)

Age: 83–65 mya
Size: 49 ft long
Weight: 5.6 tons
Location: USA: Montana; Canada: Alberta; Mexico: Baja
Food: Herbivore

Named "Lambe's lizard" in honor of Canadian paleontologist Lawrence Lambe, this was a large, duckbilled dinosaur. Its crest was forward facing and has been compared to a hatchet in shape. The purpose of its crest is subject to debate. The crest was hollow and connected to Lambeosaurus's nasal passages. It may have helped the dinosaur produce loud sounds.

Leaellynasaura (lee-ELL-in-ah-SORE-ah)

Age: Cretaceous, 105 mya
Size: 10 ft long
Weight: 200 lbs
Location: Australia
Food: Herbivore

Paleontologists Thomas Rich and Patricia-Vickers Rich discovered Leaellynasaura and named it in honor of their daughter, Leaellyn, in 1989. The part of Australia where Leaellynasaura lived was within the Antarctic Circle 105 million years ago. While warmer then, long cycles of darkness and cold still occurred. Leaellynasaura's existence was the first discovery to show that some dinosaurs had adapted to these conditions. Perhaps Leaellynasaura was a warm-blooded creature. It had large eyes, which helped it see well during the dark periods.

Maiasaura (My-ah-SORE-ah)

Age: 77–76 mya
Size: 30 ft long
Weight: 2.9 tons
Location: USA: Montana
Food: Herbivore

Paleontologists Jack Horner and Robert Makela found and named the "good mother lizard" in an area carpeted with fossilized dinosaur nests. Juvenile skeletons have also been found at the site, demonstrating that Maiasaura may have cared for its young for some time. Some of the babies had weak limb bones, but worn teeth, suggesting that the mothers brought food to the nest to feed their young. Fossil records also indicate that Maiasaura may have herded in groups that numbered in the thousands. Maiasaura had a duck-like beak and self-sharpening teeth in the cheeks of its powerful jaws. Since the first discovery, scientists have found thousands more fossils.

Astronaut Loren Acton brought a Maiasaura fossil along for the ride on a space shuttle mission in 1985. Maiasaura became the first dinosaur to visit space.

Mei (my)

Age: 125 mya
Size: 16 in long
Weight: 1 lb
Location: China
Food: Carnivore

About the size of a duck, and with the appearance of a chicken, Mei was a feathered ancestor to modern birds. It feasted on a diet that probably included insects and small animals. The name means "sleeping soundly" because the fossil remains were resting peacefully with the head tucked under a wing. The dinosaur probably died of suffocation from volcanic gases.

Microraptor (MY-crow-RAP-tore)

Age: 128–124 mya
Size: 3 ft long
Weight: 2 lbs
Location: China
Food: Carnivore

Described by paleontologist Xu Xing in 2003, the number of fossilized skeletons is close to 300. Microraptor was one of the smallest dinosaurs yet found, and its name reflects its size: "small thief." Although not a true bird, Microraptor was very close in appearance. It had two sets of wings, both covered with feathers. However, it did not have the flight muscles needed for a powerful takeoff. Scientists think it may have glided from treetop to treetop. Unlike birds, Microraptor had teeth and a bony tail. The tail had a fan of feathers near the end. Xu Xing discovered one fossil with the skeleton of a bird in its stomach area.

Minmi (MIN-me)

Age: 119–113 mya
Size: 10 ft long
Weight: 660 lbs
Location: Australia
Food: Herbivore

Minmi's head resembled that of a modern snapping turtle. As an ankylosaur, it was heavily armored with plates at the back of the neck and small scutes protecting the belly. Larger scutes guarded the shoulders while rows of smaller scutes ran along the back and sides of the dinosaur. A ridge of thorn-shaped triangular plates descended down the tail. The first skeleton was found near Minmi Crossing, from which the dinosaur receives its name. One skeleton had the remains of a final meal: seeds, leaves, and small fruit.

Muttaburrasaurus (MOO-tah-BUH-ruh-SORE-us)

Age: 100–98 mya
Size: 26 ft long
Weight: 2.7 tons
Location: Australia
Food: Herbivore

Muttaburrasaurus had a bone formation on its snout that gave it the look of an arched nose. Its nasal passages were wide, perhaps for making loud sounds or for helping warm the air it breathed. Another possibility is that the large passages gave Muttaburrasaurus a keen sense of smell. This dinosaur emerged from the ground near the Queensland town of Muttaburra. Cattle disturbed the bones and scattered them as they grazed. People took home the bones they found. Eventually, many were returned to paleontologists digging the rest of the skeleton.

Nemegtosaurus (nem-EGG-toe-SORE-us)

Age: 80–65 mya
Size: Possibly up to 50 ft long
Weight: Unknown
Location: Mongolia
Food: Herbivore

Named for the Nemegt Basin in the Gobi Desert where the first Nemegtosaurus find occurred. Only a partial skull was found, so size estimates have proven difficult to make. The front portion of the jaw had small, peg-shaped teeth. The head sloped forward. Nemegtosaurus likely had a long neck for feeding in tall trees.

Nigersaurus (NEE-jer-SORE-us)

Age: 119–99 mya
Size: 30 ft long
Weight: 1.9 tons
Location: Niger
Food: Herbivore

Walking on all fours with a long tail and a fairly long neck, Nigersaurus looked much like a typical sauropod—except for its mouth, which was shaped like a flat vacuum cleaner nozzle. In addition, the bones in its skull were so thin they were almost clear. That gave Nigersaurus a very light load to bear. In 2007, paleontologists studied the skull and its relation to the animal's posture. They discovered that Nigersaurus kept its head low to the ground. It fed by sweeping its head back and forth over low-growing vegetation, tearing it loose, and sucking it in like a vacuum.

Ornithomimus (OR-nith-oh-MIME-us)

Age: 75–65 mya
Size: 15 ft long
Weight: 300 lbs
Location: Western USA, Canada
Food: Omnivore

The "bird mimic" resembled an ostrich. It had a larger brain than many other dinosaurs of the time, but was not nearly as smart as an ostrich. Ornithomimus's bones were hollow and its legs long, making it a fast runner. Its flexible tail allowed Ornithomimus to make quick, sharp turns even when moving at top speed. Some scientists estimate it may have been able to reach speeds of up to 43 mph, about the same as an ostrich.

Ouranosaurus (ooh-RAN-uh-SORE-us)

Age: 115 mya
Size: 24 ft long
Weight: 4 tons
Location: Niger
Food: Herbivore

A sail rose across Ouranosaurus's back, supported by a series of bony blades. Africa was hot and dry during the Cretaceous Period, so the sail may have helped it regulate its body temperature. Many sail-backed dinosaurs lived in hot climates. Ouranosaurus's head was long and its wrists were strong, but not quite strong enough to grip. Its name means "brave lizard."

Pachycephalosaurus (pack-ee-sef-ah-low-SORE-us)

Age: 68–65 mya
Size: 15 ft long
Weight: 990 lbs
Location: USA: Montana, South Dakota, Wyoming
Food: Herbivore

Pachycephalosaurus's name means "thick-headed lizard"—and for good reason. The dome of its skull was a thick, solid bone, every bit as thick as a bowling ball. It may have used that tough skull for butting heads with males. Its stout backbone seems to have been built to absorb shock, which supports the head butting theory. It also bore some bony spikes on its snout and near the top of its head. Its teeth appear to suggest it ate less tough, easier to digest plant material.

Pachyrhinosaurus (pack-ee-RHINE-oh-SORE-us)

Age: 73–70 mya
Size: 26 ft long
Weight: 3.9 tons
Location: USA: Alaska
Food: Herbivore

More important than this plant eater's appearance was where it was found. During its time, Alaska was even farther north than it is today, which means that this herbivore had somehow adapted to living in freezing polar temperatures while maintaining a diet that included an enormous amount of vegetation. Its name means "thick nosed lizard" for the massive bump it wore in place of a nasal horn like Triceratops.

Panoplosaurus (pan-OP-luh-SORE-us)

Age: 76–73 mya
Size: 23 ft long
Weight: 3.5 tons
Location: USA: Montana; Canada: Alberta
Food: Herbivore

Built like a tank, Panoplosaurus had bony plates covering most all of its body. The plates on its shoulders, head, neck, and sides also had bony spikes protruding from them. Panoplosaurus's name means "totally armored lizard," and that certainly seems appropriate. It had four short legs and a stiff tail.

Parasaurolophus (PAR-ah-SORE-oh-LOAF-us)

Age: 76–73 mya
Size: 30 ft long
Weight: 2.4 tons
Location: Western USA to New Mexico, Canada
Food: Herbivore

Parasaurolophus's name means "near lizard crest," at least partially because of its most distinguishing feature: a long, tube-like crest on the top of its head. Paleontologists debated the purpose of the crest for years, but it now seems most likely that Parasaurolophus used the device for making sounds, perhaps as a means of communicating with herds. The crest had hollow tubes inside and would have made loud, trumpet-like noises. Parasaurolophus had a thick, muscular build for pushing through thick undergrowth. Its tail was stiff, so it is not likely Parasaurolophus would have swung it side-to-side for quick turns.

Pentaceratops (Pen-ta-SERRA-tops)

Age: 73–75 mya
Size: 20 ft long
Weight: 8 tons
Location: USA: New Mexico
Food: Herbivore

An enormous head with a huge neck frill are among Pentaceratops's most striking features. Fragments reassembled into a complete skull measure 10 feet in length— the longest skull of any known land animal ever. Pentaceratops's name means "five-horned face." It had one large, rhinoceros-like horn on its snout, two more above the eyes, and two small horns, one on each cheek. It may have used these horns to charge attacking predators as a means of defending itself.

Psittacosaurus (SIT-ah-coe-SORE-us)

Age: 126–100 mya
Size: 5 ft long
Weight: 33 lbs
Location: Russia, Mongolia, China
Food: Herbivore

The "parrot lizard" was a two-legged plant eater that, as a genus, managed to be around for more than 25 million years. It had a short head that ended in a parrot-like beak. The beak had a pointed end for cutting, and Psittacosaurus's teeth were strong, suggesting it ate the tougher plants that many other herbivores overlooked. Its defense was most likely to flee or hide as predators approached. Two fossilized baby Psittacosaurus skeletons were found, each about the size of a modern songbird.

Saltasaurus (SALT-ah-SORE-us)

Age: 83–79 mya
Size: 40 ft long
Weight: 7.7 tons
Location: Argentina
Food: Herbivore

Although a complete skeleton is yet to be found, paleontologists have found enough bones to realize that Saltasaurus had a superior defense system. Its back was covered in a tough armor with bony studs. Because this sauropod was small compared to others, it may have needed the extra protection armor provided. The tail was long and flexible with interlocking bones and moveable joints. This gave the tail a whiplash ability, which may have also been used as a defense mechanism. The name means "Salta lizard" after the area in which it was first discovered.

Sauropelta (SORE-oh-PELT-ah)

Age: 116–91 mya
Size: 25 ft long
Weight: 3 tons
Location: USA: Montana, Wyoming
Food: Herbivore

Sauropelta looked very much like its relative, Ankylosaurus, but it lacked horns and a tail club. Its body, except for its underbelly, was covered in studded armor plates. All of this protection gave Sauropelta its name, which means "shielded lizard." Its defense strategy was probably to crouch low and hope its armor was enough to discourage predators. Its short legs likely were not enough to allow it to run from danger. Its beak was toothless, but it had cheek teeth for chewing the low-growing vegetation it ate.

Sauroposeidon (SORE-oh-poe-SIGH-don)

Age: 118–110 mya
Size: 100 ft long
Weight: 59 tons
Location: USA: Oklahoma
Food: Herbivore

Laying claim as the tallest dinosaur, Sauroposeidon stood as tall as a six-story building. Its vertebrae were so large—the biggest one is more than 4.5 feet tall—that they were first mistakenly thought to be tree trunks. The first discovery was by a dog handler at a state prison in Oklahoma in 1994. The name means "Poseidon's lizard" after the mythical god of the sea and earthquakes.

Segnosaurus (SEG-no-SORE-us)

Age: 90 mya
Size: 20 ft long
Weight: 1.2 tons
Location: Mongolia
Food: Herbivore

Mongolian paleontologist Altangerel Perle gave Segnosaurus its name, meaning "slow lizard," in 1979. This creature was a theropod, but one that evolved to eat plant material rather than meat. Skull fragments indicate that the jaw was turned downward. Segnosaurus also had extremely long, curved claws on its hands. These may have been for defense, but they also served to pull down branches and strip leaves.

Sinornithosaurus (sine-ORE-nith-oh-SORE-us)

Age: 124–122 mya

Size: 3 ft long

Weight: 3.5 lbs

Location: China

Food: Carnivore

Given a name that means, "Chinese bird lizard," it is unlikely that Sinornithosaurus could actually fly. Although its body was covered in feathers, it was too heavy to fly. As a predator, Sinornithosaurus probably caught and ate small mammals and baby dinosaurs. Some scientists claim that Sinornithosaurus was venomous, citing the grooves in its fangs. Others argue the opposite, pointing out that other theropods also had grooved teeth.

Sinornithosaurus is one of the first dinosaurs examined for its feather colors.

Sinosauropteryx (SIGH-no-sore-OP-ter-ix)

Age: 130–125 mya

Size: 4 ft long

Weight: 5.5 lbs

Location: China

Food: Carnivore

Discovered in the Liaoning Quarry in 1996, Sinosauropteryx was the first feathered dinosaur ever found. Fossil evidence clearly showed simple feathers over its back and sides. This fluffy down was not capable of allowing flight, so they may have been used for warmth or display. Like Sinornithosaurus, scientists have studied the color pigments left behind in Sinosauropteryx bones to get an idea of the dinosaur's colors. Its name means "Chinese lizard wing." Fossils included some of its internal organs, unlaid eggs, and its stomach contents (the skeleton of a small mammal).

Spinosaurus (SPINE-oh-SORE-us)

Age: 112–97 mya

Size: 59 ft long

Weight: 8.8 tons

Location: Egypt, Morocco

Food: Carnivore

Closely related to Baryonyx, the "spine lizard" was the largest carnivorous dinosaur ever found, even larger than Tyrannosaurus. It had a tall sail on its back, supported by spines up to 6 feet tall projecting from its vertebrae. Like other sail-bearing dinosaurs, it may have helped regulate body temperature. But at least one paleontologist, Cristiano Dal Sasso, thinks Spinosaurus may have used its sail to cast shade over water, attracting the fish it would catch and eat. Its long, narrow jaws were ideal for catching fish, but it probably hunted on land as well as in the water, consuming turtles, smaller dinosaurs, and birds along with fish.

Wastebasket Genus

Sometimes, especially in the early days of paleontology, fossil hunters mistakenly included new finds in an old classification. Megalosaurus was an early wastebasket genus at one time. The problem was that insufficient study led to missing key information. As a result, many different dinosaurs got lumped into one genus. Once scientists slowed down and began a closer study of the fossils, small peculiarities emerged. The shape of a bone might have been slightly different, or the teeth may have had a different shape. Only then did scientists begin creating different names for each dinosaur they had once thought were the same. As naming rules go, the first that received the name kept it, so each dinosaur pulled out of the wastebasket genus had to get a different name.

Struthiomimus (STROO-thee-oh-MIME-us)

Age: 76–74 mya
Size: 13 ft long
Weight: 330 lbs
Location: Canada: Alberta
Food: Omnivore

The "ostrich mimic" was indeed built much like today's ostriches. Its arms were longer and its hands more powerful than its relative, Ornithomimus. Long claws tipped fingers that were probably not able to grasp. Struthiomimus had a long neck and long legs. Its flexible tail likely gave it excellent balance and helped it achieve running speeds of 40 mph with short bursts up to 50 mph. Gastroliths (grinding stones) found in the belly of fossils indicate that Struthiomimus was a plant eater. However, it also had a sharp beak, suggesting it may have also preyed on small animals, lizards, and insects.

Styracosaurus (sty-RACK-oh-SORE-us)

Age: 75–72 mya
Size: 20 ft long
Weight: 2.7 tons
Location: Canada: Alberta;
USA: Montana
Food: Herbivore

A large and showy heart-shaped neck frill had 6 long spikes along the edges in a fan-shaped pattern. Some of the bony spikes measured up to 2 feet long. Styracosaurus also had a long, pointed nose horn. These features earned Styracosaurus its name, which means "spiked lizard." Paleontologists believe that Styracosaurus males may have had thrashing contests similar to those of modern-day deer. Some fossils indicate that injuries occurred during these contests. Styracosaurus also had a large snout and enormous nostrils, which might suggest an excellent sense of smell. Bone beds where several skeletons are found together show that Styracosaurus traveled in herds.

Suchomimus (soo-ko-MIME-us)

Age: 121–112 mya
Size: 36 ft long
Weight: 4.9 tons
Location: Niger
Food: Carnivore

Suchomimus means "crocodile mimic," a name referring to its long snout and sharp, pointed teeth. A set of long teeth clustered at the end of the snout, while more than 100 backward slanted teeth lined the edges of the jaw. The front teeth let Suchomimus snatch fish, while the jaw teeth prevented the prey's escape. Suchomimus hunted in swamps that existed in Cretaceous Africa, probably hunting or scavenging land animals as well as fish. A nearly complete skeleton emerged from the sands of the Sahara Desert in 1997, a large sickle-shaped claw being one of the first fossils spotted. Wind erosion exposed part of the skeleton, but scientists moved more than 16 tons of rock and sand before the entire skeleton was freed.

Tarbosaurus (TAR-bow-SORE-us)

Age: 70–69 mya
Size: 31 ft long
Weight: 3.9 tons
Location: Northern China, Mongolia
Food: Carnivore

Tarbosaurus, the "dreadful lizard," was so closely related to Tyrannosaurus that some paleontologists think it should be a Tyrannosaurus species instead of its own genus. Tarbosaurus was almost as large as its American cousin, but it had a more slender skull and even tinier arms than Tyrannosaurus. Its jaws were powerful, and Tarbosaurus likely used them to crush its victims before swallowing chunks whole.

Tenontosaurus (ten-NON-toe-SORE-us)

Age: 115–108 mya

Size: 25 ft long

Weight: 2 tons

Location: Western North America

Food: Herbivore

Tenontosaurus's tail made up the majority of its length. A network of strong tendons in the tail ensured that Tenontosaurus kept it off the ground. The name means "sinew lizard." Tenon is the Latin name for sinew. Many remains were found with teeth belonging to a small predator named Deinonychus, suggesting that the carnivore hunted Tenontosaurus, maybe in packs in order to bring it down.

Therizinosaurus (THERRY-zin-oh-SORE-us)

Age: 70 mya

Size: 33 ft long

Weight: 4.9 tons

Location: Mongolia

Food: Herbivore

Imposing claws up to 2 feet long originally led scientists to believe that Therizinosaurus was a predator. But the discovery of Segnosaurus helped scientists understand that the larger Therizinosaurus was also a plant eater. They think the giant claws were a means of shredding plant material and cutting down small vegetation. Other fossil discoveries revealed a toothless beak, a feature often found in plant eaters. The Gobi Desert, where Therizinosaurus discoveries were made, was a warm, wet woodland with tall trees at the time Therizinosaurus roamed the area.

Titanosaurus (tie-TAN-oh-SORE-us)

Age: 80–65 mya
Size: 60 ft long
Weight: 16 tons
Location: India
Food: Herbivore

Richard Lydekker named this dinosaur in 1877 with a term meaning "titanic lizard." It was a huge dinosaur with a long tail and long neck. After the discovery of its tailbones, scientists at the time named an entirely new family they called titanosaurs. But since that time, many other dinosaur discoveries revealed features not at all unique to Titanosaurus. This may be a mistaken genus. However, because no skull has been found yet, paleontologists cannot say for certain whether Titanosaurus is unique.

Triceratops (try-SERRA-tops)

Age: 68–65 mya
Size: 30 ft long
Weight: 10.8 tons
Location: USA: Montana, North Dakota, South Dakota, Wyoming
Food: Herbivore

At the time when Triceratops lived, the western portion of North America was cool and dry with thick forests and tall trees. An inland sea to the east, where much of the Midwestern United States is today, was shrinking with each passing year. Triceratops was among the last and the most numerous of the horned dinosaurs. It ate vegetation in those forests and tried to avoid attacks from Tyrannosaurus, which preyed on Triceratops. Some fossils show Tyrannosaurus tooth marks on them. Dozens of skulls have emerged from western rocks over the years, each found individually, suggesting that Triceratops did not often travel in herds. A beak and a large, broad neck frill were prominent Triceratops features. Its name means "three-horned face." It had two long horns, one above each eye, and a shorter horn near the tip of its snout.

Troodon (TROH-oh-don)

Age: 75–65 mya
Size: 6.5 ft long
Weight: 110 lbs
Location: USA: Alaska, Montana, Wyoming; Canada: Alberta
Food: Omnivore

Troodon had a large brain compared to its body size, about six times heavier than those of comparably sized dinosaurs. Many paleontologists believe that Troodon was the most intelligent dinosaur to have existed. It had forward-facing eyes that provided excellent vision like humans and strong night vision. Troodon also had excellent hearing. With these tools, it may have attacked sleeping dinosaurs, killing them with its large, sickle-shaped toe claws and sharp teeth. Troodon probably also ate snakes, lizards, small mammals, and vegetation.

The name means "wounding tooth" from the single, serrated tooth Joseph Leidy found in 1856. Troodon actually sported about 120 teeth, which were hooked rearward. It was quick and agile, with long, slender limbs. Nesting sites found in Montana held about 24 eggs and were around 6 feet wide.

Tsintaosaurus (sin-dow-SORE-us)

Age: 70 mya
Size: 33 ft long
Weight: 2.9 tons
Location: China
Food: Herbivore

Tsintaosaurus was a duck-billed dinosaur with an odd-looking skull ornament, a solid shaft of bone that gave it the nickname, "unicorn dinosaur." Its actual name means "Tsintao lizard," after the name of the town near its discovery. The purpose of its bone shaft is unknown.

Tyrannosaurus (tie-RAN-oh-SORE-us)

Age: 68–65 mya

Size: 39 ft long

Weight: 5.9 tons

Location: USA: Colorado, Montana, New Mexico, Wyoming; Canada: Alberta, Saskatchewan

Food: Carnivore

Perhaps in awe of its size and fierceness, Tyrannosaurus is the only dinosaur popularly known by its full genus and species name: Tyrannosaurus rex, sometimes shortened to T. rex. First discovered in 1902 by Barnum Brown, it gained immediate public recognition as newspapers headlined the story.

Tyrannosaurus terrorized North America over the last few million years that dinosaurs dominated the planet. The "king of the tyrant lizards" had powerful jaws 5 feet long with 60 banana-shaped teeth and crushing force. Tyrannosaurus could snatch up its prey, snap the bones and swallow a meal whole or tear off enormous chunks of flesh. Should it break a tooth in the process, it simply grew another one to take its place.

It walked on strong hind legs, but could only achieve speeds of 15 to 25 mph, enough to chase slower herbivores such as Triceratops. Paleontologists have also found evidence of pack hunting in Tyrannosaurs. When not giving chase to prey, Tyrannosaurus may have scavenged food from dead carcasses. It roamed with its back level to the ground, its head raised slightly and its body balanced with a stiff tail. Tyrannosaurus had spaces in its skull bones that helped lighten its weight. The brain was long and narrow with large regions that controlled hearing, sight, and smell, all likely heightened senses.

Utahraptor (YOU-tah-RAP-tore)

Age: 130–125 mya
Size: 23 ft long
Weight: 1,100 lbs
Location: USA: Utah
Food: Carnivore

First discovered by American paleontologist Jim Jensen in 1975, a more detailed study began in 1991, after a large claw emerged. This fully feathered dinosaur had long sickle-shaped talons it used to kill its prey. One of these claws measured 9 inches long. What this predator lacked in size, it made up for with its fierce nature. Utahraptor was named for the state in which its remains were discovered.

Sue Hendrickson found the most famous Tyrannosaurus skeleton in 1990, and it bears her first name. The fossil resides at the Field Museum of Natural History in Chicago, having sold at auction for $8.3 million in 1997.

Velociraptor (vel-OSS-ih-RAP-tore)

Age: 83–70 mya
Size: 8 ft long
Weight: 33 lbs
Location: Mongolia
Food: Carnivore

Velociraptor was a fast and an aggressive hunter, earning it a name that means "speedy thief." Not at all like the Velociraptor portrayed in the movie *Jurassic Park*, the real dinosaur was small and covered with feathers rather than scales. Those feathers did not support flight and were probably a means of staying warm.

Velociraptor was equipped with sharp teeth and knife-like claws. It could jab its claw into a victim to kill it, then tear it apart with its narrow jaws lined with about 80 teeth. Velociraptor may have been a pack hunter, jumping on its prey with all four limbs extended. Small dinosaurs, lizards, and mammals were likely on the menu.

A spectacular fossil find pulled from Mongolia in 1971 has a Velociraptor locked into a fierce fight with a Protoceratops. The Velociraptor has one of its killing claws embedded in the Protoceratops's neck as its hand slashes at the face. The victim has the predator's arm locked into its beak. Scientists think the two dinosaurs killed each other in battle before their bodies were covered during a sandstorm.

DIGGING DEEPER

What Color Were Dinosaurs?

From paleontologists to artists to anyone fascinated with dinosaurs, that question has probably come up more than once. Because no one was around to observe and describe dinosaurs, it's a question that had more guesses than facts. Until recently.

In early 2010, scientists began studying tiny cells called melanosomes that they found in the feather impressions left behind by dinosaurs. Melanosomes are so small that 100 of them could fit across the width of a single human hair. These structures carry pigments, or colors, and researchers thought they might be able to find out something about dinosaur colors from the melanosomes they found.

Using an electron microscope capable of magnifying the structures 500,000 times, researchers could see the shapes of each melanosome. Shapes indicate colors. Blacks and greys were cigar-shaped, and reds, browns, and yellows were more round.

Some feathered dinosaur fossils were loaded with bands of melanosomes. As a result, scientists could determine color patterns on some dinosaur species, such as the blacks, whites, and reds found on Anchiornis.

Melanosomes account for some colors, but not all of them. Other cells carry pigments for pink, deep reds, and orange, but those do not last during fossilization. Dinosaurs that did not have feathers are also a problem because their fossilized scales do not seem to hold cells with pigments in them. Maybe the future will hold some new means of accurately determining the colors of all dinosaurs.

Ichthyovenator

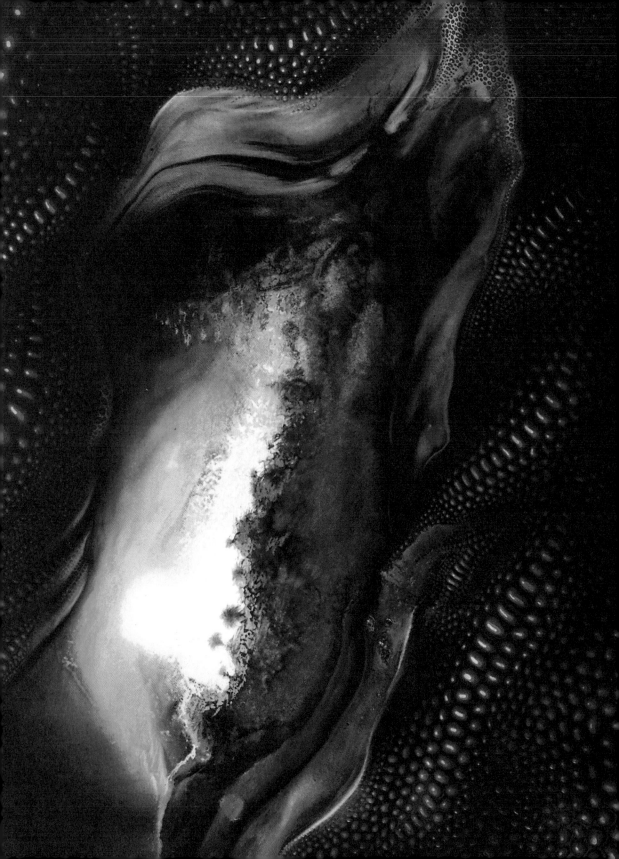

Other Animals of the Mesozoic Era

Dinosaurs were not the only creatures that lived during the Mesozoic Era. Dinosaurs were strictly land animals. They neither flew nor swam the seas, but other animals did. Flying reptiles patrolled the skies, while toothed and ferocious aquatic reptiles ruled the oceans. Toward the end of the Cretaceous Period, some of these reptiles and many mammals were getting more successful. Dinosaurs found more and more competition in the world.

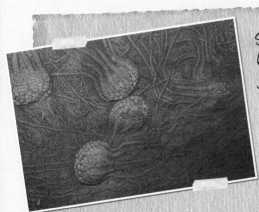

Some familiar animals of today go back to the age of the dinosaurs. Jellyfish began life long before dinosaurs arrived, and they outlasted them by millions more years. Jellyfish have existed for more than 400 million years. Corals may be fragile, but they have figured out ways to survive since the Mesozoic Era. Fossil records show that some prehistoric fish fed on squids, and snails also appear in fossil form. Turtles were also present, although much larger than today's versions. One, Archelon, had a shell that was 13 feet long, around three times bigger than the largest modern turtle.

Fish and Marine Life

Hybodus (hi-BODE-us)

Age: Permian, 254–65 mya
Size: 6 ft long
Weight: 100–200 lbs
Location: Worldwide
Food: Carnivore

Looked much like modern sharks. A long spine in front of the dorsal fin was distinctive and may have been used for defense, or to help Hybodus cut through the water with ease. Its front teeth were sharp and made for gripping prey, while the back teeth were more blunt for crushing hard seashells.

Leedsichthys (LEEDS-ick-this)

Age: Jurassic, 176–161 mya
Size: 30 ft long
Weight: 1–2 tons
Location: Europe, Chile
Food: Carnivore

Larger than today's killer whales, this was a filter feeder that did not hunt prey. Instead, it sucked in huge amounts of water, using its gills to sift the shrimp and other small marine animals for food. One fossil had clear bite marks from Pliosaurus, which hunted and attacked Leedsichthys.

Lepidotes (lepi-DOE-tees)

Age: Jurassic, 160–140 mya

Size: 25 lbs

Weight: 6 ft long

Location: Lakes of the Northern Hemisphere

Food: Carnivore

Fossil impressions show that Lepidotes was covered in thick, diamond-shaped scales. It fed by pushing out its jaws and inhaling shellfish to crush in its jaws. Lepidotes teeth are often found in England, where they have the unusual name of "toad-stones." Centuries ago, people thought the stones were from the heads of living toads, and the name stuck.

Macropoma (mack-roe-POME-ah)

Age: Cretaceous, 70 mya

Size: 22 in long

Weight: Less than 10 lbs

Location: England, Czech Republic

Food: Carnivore

Scientists once thought this might be a link between fish and land animals because Macropoma had fleshy fins it could move like arms or legs. Thought to have been extinct for millions of years, fishermen were shocked to catch one in South Africa in 1938.

Pliosaurus (PLY-oh-SORE-us)

Age: Jurassic, 147 mya

Size: 39 ft long

Weight: 25 tons

Location: Norway

Food: Carnivore

This creature could rival sharks and even Tyrannosaurus. Its enormous mouth had foot-long, spiked teeth and jaws that could crush victims with much more force than T. rex. Pliosaurus swam the seas using its front flippers, then used its rear flippers for a sudden burst of speed when approaching a victim.

Xiphactinus (zye-FACK-tee-nuss)

Age: Cretaceous, 112–70 mya

Size: 20 ft long

Weight: 500 lbs

Location: North America

Food: Carnivore

A long, lean, muscular body made Xiphactinus a strong swimmer. Its massive mouth allowed it to swallow prey whole. One fossil had the skeleton of a 7-foot-long fish inside the belly. Scientists think it may have killed the Xiphactinus as it thrashed inside the body.

Ammonites from the Cretaceous Period

Flying Reptiles

Dawndraco kanzai

Pterosaurs were close relatives of the dinosaurs, but were reptiles. They flew, but were not related to birds. They appeared about 215 million years ago, during the late Triassic Period, and they survived until the end of the Cretaceous Period 65 million years ago. The early ones were small, with narrow wings and long tails. The tails helped pterosaurs control their flight pattern. By the Cretaceous Period, pterosaurs had grown larger. Many of their fossils were discovered along coastal regions, suggesting a diet of fish that may have been supplemented with insects. Their large eyes indicate keen vision. Pterosaurs flew with wings that resembled those of modern bats. A skin membrane stretched from an elongated fourth finger to the hind legs.

Dimorphodon (die-MORE-foe-don)

Age: Jurassic, 197–195 mya
Size: 4-foot wingspan
Weight: 5 lbs
Location: British Isles
Food: Carnivore

Mary Anning made the first discovery of this pterosaur, but the skeleton lacked a skull. Later discoveries showed a large head that made up almost a third of the total body length. Its name means "two-form tooth," referring to two different types of teeth. This was an unusual feature in pterosaurs. Its front fangs and back grinding pegs indicate a diet of insects and small animals rather than fish. Its beak was large and looked similar to that of a modern puffin.

Eudimorphodon (YOU-die-MORE-foe-don)

Age: Triassic, 210 mya
Size: 3-foot wingspan
Weight: 22 lbs
Location: Italy, Germany
Food: Carnivore

One of the earliest known pterosaurs, Eudimorphodon had a short neck and a long tail. These features changed in later species. The tail had a diamond-shaped flap that Eudimorphodon used to maneuver as it skimmed along above a lake in search of fish. Its long, tooth-lined jaws were well equipped to grasp slippery prey. Some fossils had scales in the stomach region.

Pteranodon (ter-RAN-oh-don)

Age: Cretaceous, 88–80 mya
Size: 23–30-foot wingspan
Weight: 55 lbs
Location: North America
Food: Carnivore

Pteranodon had a slender and pointed beak for scooping fish. These flying reptiles hunted in large flocks as they flew over Cretaceous Period oceans. It had a long crest on its head.

Pterodactylus (terr-oh-DACK-till-us)

Age: Jurassic, 150–148 mya
Size: 2-foot wingspan
Weight: 10 lbs
Location: Germany
Food: Carnivore

Its body was only a foot long, with a short tail but a longer neck than its predecessors. The body build allowed for better, more controlled flight. It also had a rear-facing crest on its head. Pterodactylus is the earliest and the most well-known of pterosaur discoveries. Its long jaws tapered to a spear-shaped tip that was ideal for catching fish. The first fossils were described in 1784. Since then, dozens more have been located.

Quetzalcoatlus (kay-et-SAL-coat-luss)

Age: Cretaceous, 70–65 mya
Size: 40–46-foot wingspan
Weight: 55 lbs
Location: USA
Food: Carnivore

With a wingspan larger than that of a small airplane, Quetzalcoatlus was the largest flying reptile of its era. Fossil remains were found in Texas. Even with such a large body, its weight was around 55 pounds because of its light, hollow bones. It likely traveled long distances, soaring in search of small mammals and baby dinosaurs.

Rhamphorhynchus (RAM-foe-RINK-us)

Age: Jurassic, 150 mya
Size: 6-foot wingspan
Weight: 10 lbs
Location: Germany
Food: Carnivore

Rhamphorhynchus cruised low over lakes and rivers, snatching fish and possibly amphibians into its long, narrow jaws. Those jaws were lined with spiked teeth, and a throat pouch helped hold the catch. A large flap at the end of its tail aided with steering.

Just for Fun

Many paleontologists believe that birds are the only remaining relatives of the huge beasts that once ruled Earth. But what if a great extinction never happened at the end of the Cretaceous Period? What if dinosaurs continued to develop and evolve over the next 65 million years? What would they look like today? Would they have become highly intelligent? Would they have developed complex communications? Would the age of mammals still have occurred? Would humans still have appeared on the scene? If humans did show up, would we eventually have tamed dinosaurs the way we have horses, or cattle? What other questions might you ponder if large dinosaurs were still alive today?

Mammals

Megazostrodon

Mammals began to appear on the scene late in the Triassic Period. Early forms were very primitive and some looked more like reptiles than mammals. Most were so small they could fit in your hand. Because they had to hide from dinosaurs and other predators, they were probably nocturnal animals. They scurried about searching leaf litter for insects and sneaking into dinosaur nests to feast on eggs. Many walked on all fours and had long snouts for probing. A small hole in the skull behind each creature's eyes distinguished these animals as mammals instead of reptiles. The holes provided a passageway for jaw muscles that gave mammals a strong bite.

Eomaia (EE-oh-MY-ah)

Age: Cretaceous, 125 mya
Size: 8 in long
Weight: 1 oz
Location: China
Food: Carnivore

One well-preserved fossil is all we know of Eomaia. It was a good climber and it wore a thick coat of fur. The bones suggest it gave birth to live young rather than laying eggs and its diet likely included some small animals as well as insects.

Megazostrodon (MEG-ah-ZO-stroh-don)

Age: Jurassic, 190 mya
Size: 4 in long
Weight: 1–2 oz
Location: South Africa
Food: Carnivore

With a long snout and tail plus a slender body, Megazostrodon looked much like a shrew. An insectivore, Megazostrodon appeared to have had a relatively large brain with enlarged areas that controlled hearing and smell.

Morganucodon (MORE-gan-oo-CODE-on)

Age: Triassic, 210–180 mya
Size: 4 in long
Weight: 1–3 oz
Location: Wales, China, USA
Food: Carnivore

The first glimpse of Morganucodon was from thousands of fossilized teeth found in a quarry in Wales. Later discoveries placed Morganucodon in many other countries as well, suggesting it was a very common species across the Triassic world. Its jaw showed many features of a mammal, but maintained other features that better resembled a reptile.

How did mammals manage to survive the great extinction that wiped out the dinosaurs? The debris from a meteorite strike and volcanic eruptions likely cooled the planet, destroying vegetation. But early mammal fur provided better protection against a colder climate, and their small size meant they could survive on far less food.

Nemegtbaatar (nemt-BAY-ter)

Age: Cretaceous, 65 mya
Size: 4 in long
Weight: 2–3 oz
Location: Mongolia
Food: Possibly an omnivore

Nemegtbaatar's wide snout was peppered with holes for blood vessel passages. It looked bucktoothed, with large, forward-slanting front teeth. Nemegtbaatar resembled modern voles.

Oligokyphus (OLE-ih-go-KEY-fuss)

Age: Triassic, 227–180 mya
Size: 19 in long
Weight: 1 lb
Location: Great Britain, Germany, North America, China
Food: Herbivore

A weasel-like animal with strong teeth that indicate it ate tougher plants, seeds, and nuts. This species appeared during the Triassic Period, but was able to survive well into the Jurassic, making it a successful herbivore.

Sinoconodon (SIGH-no-CON-oh-don)

Age: Triassic, 200 mya
Size: 12 in long
Weight: 2–3 oz
Location: China
Food: Omnivore

Sinoconodon had features of both mammals and reptiles. The skeleton and skull resembled those of other mammals, but it lost and replaced teeth many times over the course of its life, much like a reptile. Its strong jaws packed a powerful bite.

Teinolophos (TIE-nuh-LOW-fuss)

Age: Cretaceous, 125 mya
Size: 4 in long
Weight: 10 oz
Location: Australia
Food: Carnivore

Only Teinolophos's lower jaw was discovered, but it indicated the strength of a potent bite. An egg layer, Teinolophos may be an early ancestor of a duckbilled platypus, one of the few modern mammals that still lays eggs.

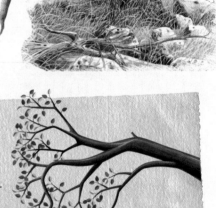

Prior to the 21st century, scientists thought dinosaurs were so dominant that early mammals did not have much opportunity to adapt to diverse conditions. More recent findings show that some mammals adapted to become tree climbers, burrowers, or water dwellers.

Zalambdalestes (ZAH-lam-da-LESS-tease)

Age: Jurassic, 80–70 mya
Size: 8 in long
Weight: 3–4 oz
Location: Mongolia
Food: Carnivore

Zalambdalestes gave live birth to well-developed young. It used the earliest known form of a placenta. Like beavers and other rodents, Zalambdalestes's teeth never stopped growing throughout its life. It likely had to chew constantly to keep them the correct size. Zalambdalestes may have hopped because its hind legs were longer than its forelegs.

Insects and Spiders

Cockroach

Insects provided an important food source for reptiles, early mammals, and smaller dinosaurs. They also helped maintain Mesozoic ecosystems by consuming dead plant and animal material. Some adapted to become specialists, such as termites that concentrated only on eating woody fibers, or bees that pollinated the flowers that arrived during the Cretaceous Period. Some of today's insects have not changed much at all from their ancestors in size, appearance, or specialty. Insects were as successful in the Mesozoic Era as they are today, and specimens have been found worldwide.

Ants

Age: Cretaceous, 110–130 mya
Number: More than 12,000 species today

Ants were still evolving during the Mesozoic Era and did not become common until later eras, after the dinosaurs disappeared. Ants evolved from wasps that managed to live in underground colonies.

Bees

Age: Cretaceous, 100 mya

Number: 20,000 species today

Before the Cretaceous period, flowering plants did not exist, so there was no need for pollinators such as bees. As some prehistoric wasps abandoned preying on insects and started sipping nectar, bees eventually evolved as an offshoot.

Beetles

Age: Permian, 260 mya

Number: About 1 million species today

Flying insects with two pairs of wings began developing hard cases instead, along with a second pair of wings. The former front wings, now cases, folded over the back wings for protection. The first flowers were probably pollinated by visiting beetles.

Cockroaches

Age: Carboniferous, 350–300 mya

Number: More than 4,500 species today

Cockroaches have not changed much in appearance from when they first arrived on the scene. They spent much of their time scurrying prehistoric forest floors for rotting plant matter. Termites eventually evolved from wood-consuming cockroaches that joined together in colonies.

Dragonflies

Age: Late Carboniferous, 300 mya
Number: More than 5,000 species today

Dragonflies were much larger than those of today, but they hunted in much the same way. Stalking prey with compound eyes, they chased, snatched the victim in the air, and consumed it while still flying. Dragonflies probably provided an important food source for insectivores and supplemented the fish diets of some pterosaurs.

Flies

Age: Triassic, 230 mya
Number: 24,000 species toady

Flies evolved with two wings and a pair of knob-like protrusions they move back and forth to control flight.

Spiders

Age: Devonian, 400 mya
Number: 35,000 species today

Lacking much hard tissue, spiders do not fossilize well. Ancient species were found trapped in amber, a transparent, golden material created from fossilized conifer tree resins. The oldest known spider web fossil is from around 100 million years ago.

Other Animals

Reptiles

Deinosuchus

Reptiles descended from early, primitive amphibians more than 300 million years ago. About 60 million years later, dinosaurs evolved from reptiles. Some early reptiles adapted to flying, while others learned to flourish in Mesozoic seas. Still other reptiles found success raiding eggs from dinosaur nests or surviving on land insects, and some spent time in the water as well as on land. As they are today, reptiles in the Mesozoic Era were a diverse group of animals that learned to adapt to ongoing changes in the world.

Dakosaurus (DACK-oh-SORE-us)

Age: Cretaceous, 165–140 mya
Size: 15 ft long
Weight: 1 ton
Location: Worldwide
Food: Carnivore

Its head looked like it could have come from a carnivorous dinosaur, but this reptile lived in the sea. Jagged teeth and a strong jaw gave it a fearsome bite. Its legs adapted to become more like paddles and a fish-like tail powered Dakosaurus through the water.

Deinosuchus (DY-no-SU-kus)

Age: Cretaceous, 70–65 mya

Size: 33 ft long

Weight: 5–10 tons

Location: Swamps of USA, Mexico

Food: Carnivore

Deinosuchus was a prehistoric alligator, and one of the largest. It was around five times larger and heavier than modern alligators. Its diet included fish and some dinosaurs. Even Tyrannosaurus fossils display teeth marks from this vicious predator. Like alligators, Deinosuchus ambushed its prey at the edge of the water, then dragged it under, drowning it.

Effigia (eff-ee-gee-ah)

Age: Triassic, 210 mya

Size: 5–10 ft long

Weight: 150–200 lbs

Location: Woodlands of western North America

Food: Omnivore

A toothless beak may have been handy for cracking open seeds. Effigia may have also included eggs and smaller animals in its diet. Its appearance was similar to that of dinosaurs. An Effigia fossil first appeared in 1947, but was not studied further until paleontologists removed the rest of the skeleton in 2006.

Elasmosaurus (ee-LAZZ-moe-SORE-us)

Age: Cretaceous, 99–65 mya
Size: 45 ft long
Weight: 3 tons
Location: Oceans of North America
Food: Carnivore

Elasmosaurus's neck was so long that scientists assembling the skeleton in 1868 placed the skull on the wrong end of the animal. A slow and deliberate swimmer, Elasmosaurus stretched its neck to the sea floor to pick off its prey, a steady diet of fish.

Exaeretodon (EX-ee-REE-toe-don)

Age: Triassic, 235–221
Size: 6 ft long
Weight: 100–200 lbs
Location: Argentina, Brazil
Food: Herbivore

Exaeretodon looked like a dog but was much larger. This early mammal-like reptile was a plant eater. By late in the Triassic Period, herbivorous reptiles like this one were on the decline because they had difficulty competing with the huge sauropod dinosaurs.

Although considered a reptile, Exaeretodon shared at least one characteristic with modern-day mammals. Juveniles did not have teeth, so they had no means of chewing tough plant material. Young Exaeretodons depended on their mothers for care and feeding until the arrival of their adult teeth.

Geosaurus (Gee-oh-SORE-us)

Age: Jurassic to Cretaceous, 165–140 mya

Size: 10 ft long

Weight: 250 lbs

Location: Europe, North America, Caribbean

Food: Carnivore

The name means "earth lizard" because scientists originally thought it was a land-dwelling reptile. Further study revealed that it spent much of its time underwater. Scientists also speculate that Geosaurus may have had a special gland, just as crocodiles do, to remove salt from its drinking water.

Ichthyosaurus (ICK-thee-oh-SORE-us)

Age: Jurassic, 199–189 mya

Size: 6 ft long

Weight: 200 lbs

Location: Oceans of British Isles, Belgium, Germany

Food: Carnivore

Slim-nosed and dolphin-like in appearance, Ichthyosaurus was not equipped with the sensitive hearing and echolocation (finding objects by bouncing sound waves off of them) that dolphins use. Large eyes helped Ichthyosaurus see well in deep water where it grabbed squid, mollusks, and fish in its needle-like teeth. Mary Anning made the first Ichthyosaurus discovery in 1811.

Kronosaurus (crow-no-SORE-us)

Age: Cretaceous, 65 mya

Size: 33 ft long

Weight: 22 tons

Location: Oceans of Australia, Colombia

Food: Carnivore

A 10-foot long head took up nearly a third of Kronosaurus's body. It was one of the largest reptiles in the sea. Huge teeth in powerful jaws allowed it to grasp its prey.

Leptosuchus (LEP-toe-SOOK-us)

Age: Triassic, 220–205 mya

Size: 39 ft long

Weight: 2 tons

Location: Arizona, Texas, New Mexico

Food: Carnivore

Not a true crocodile, Leptosuchus sure looked like one. It was part of a reptile family that developed a form similar to crocodiles, but was unrelated. Leptosuchus lived in Triassic lakes and rivers where it ate fish and probably land animals.

Liopleurodon (LIE-oh-PLOOR-oh-don)

Age: Jurassic, 165–150 mya

Size: 16–23 ft long

Weight: 3 tons

Location: Oceans of British Isles, France, Russia, Germany

Food: Carnivore

Liopleurodon was a marine reptile and a mighty carnivore. Its jaws were so large and powerful that it could have taken a car in its mouth and bitten it in two with no problem. Scientists think it may have located prey with a strong sense of smell.

Mosasaurus (MOSE-ah-SORE-us)

Age: Cretaceous, 70–65 mya

Size: 50 ft long

Weight: 15 tons

Location: Oceans of USA, Belgium, Japan, Netherlands, New Zealand

Food: Carnivore

Even though it had flippers, Mosasaurus was not a fast swimmer over long distances. It did have quick bursts of speed to pursue prey. Mosasaurus tooth marks on turtle fossils suggests it may have been a hunter in shallow waters where light was stronger.

Nothosaurus (no-tho-SORE-us)

Age: Triassic, 240–210 mya

Size: 4–13 ft long

Weight: 150–200 lbs

Location: Europe, North Africa, Russia, China

Food: Carnivore

A hunter in water, Nothosaurus rested on shore. Its incredibly long teeth interlocked like a cage for trapping fish. It had a long and powerful tail, like otters, and used it to swim and make sharp turns in water.

Ophthalmosaurus (off-THAL-moe-SORE-us)

Age: Jurassic, 165–150 mya

Size: 16 ft long

Weight: 1 ton

Location: Oceans of Europe, North America, Argentina

Food: Carnivore

The "eye lizard" had the biggest eyes of any prehistoric beast when compared to the size of its overall body. Its entire skull was nearly filled by its eyes. Low light conditions in the deeper parts of Jurassic oceans were not a problem for Ophthalmosaurus.

Paleontologists studying Ophthalmosaurus believe it could dive to depths of 1,600 feet or more and stay under for as many as 20 minutes. This ability allowed Ophthalmosaurus to escape predators.

Other Animals

Pachypleurosaurus (PACK-ee-ploo-roe-SORE-us)

Age: Triassic, 225 mya
Size: 3 ft long
Weight: 15–20 lbs
Location: Italy, Switzerland
Food: Carnivore

With its legs held tight to its slender body, Pachypleurosaurus looked like a snake. Its tail enabled it to dart quickly if necessary. Most of the time, it swam by moving its body in waves.

Placerias (plah-SEE-ree-as)

Age: Triassic, 220–215 mya
Size: 6–11 ft long
Weight: 1 ton
Location: USA
Food: Herbivore

Weighing in at 2,300 pounds, Placerias had a similar weight and build as hippopotamus. It was likely a herd animal because more than 40 skeletons were found in one spot.

Platecarpus (PLAT-uh-CAR-pus)

Age: Cretaceous, 85–80 mya
Size: 14 ft long
Weight: 200–300 lbs
Location: Worldwide
Food: Carnivore

A very abundant species that died off in the mass extinction that took the dinosaurs, Platecarpus propelled itself through water like an undulating snake.

Plesiosaurus (PLEH-see-oh-SORE-us)

Age: Jurassic, 200 mya

Size: 10–15 ft long

Weight: 1,000 lbs

Location: Oceans of British Isles, Germany

Food: Carnivore

An aquatic reptile with a long neck and a body shaped like that of a turtle. Flippers propelled it in water. Its tail was so short that it likely had little use in swimming. Plesiosaurus fed by swinging its head from one side to the other as it swam through schools of fish.

Rhomaleosaurus (ROME-alley-oh-SORE-us)

Age: Jurassic, 200–195 mya

Size: 15–21 ft long

Weight: 2.5 tons

Location: Coastal water around England, Germany

Food: Carnivore

Rhomaleosaurus flapped four powerful flippers as a means of moving through the water. It had great eyesight and a keen sense of smell for locating prey. Miners discovered Rhomaleosaurus bones while digging in England in 1848.

Shastasaurus (SHAS-tah-SORE-us)

Age: Triassic, 210 mya
Size: 69 ft long
Weight: 75 tons
Location: USA, Canada, China
Food: Carnivore

The size of a whale, it had a stubby, toothless snout, and a slender body. Its skull shape indicates it fed by sucking in water and food, which consisted of mollusks and fish. The first remains were found near Mount Shasta in California.

Shonisaurus (SHON-ee-sore-us)

Age: Triassic, 225–208 mya
Size: Up to 70 ft long
Weight: 30 tons
Location: Oceans near North America
Food: Carnivore

Shonisaurus had the enormous body of a whale and the long, slender snout of a dolphin. It had large eyes, suggesting it was a deep diver, and no teeth, indicating a soft diet of squid. One 70-foot specimen makes Shonisaurus the largest marine reptile ever discovered.

Sinokannemeyeria (SIGH-no-CAN-eh-my-AIR-ee-ah)

Age: Triassic, 235 mya

Size: 6 ft long

Weight: 250 lbs

Location: China

Food: Herbivore

Tusks plus strong forelegs built for digging helped Sinokannemeyeria expose the tough roots it ate. Sinokannemeyeria also had a long snout and a massive head along with a huge stomach region to hold the large organs needed to digest the roots and tough vegetation in its diet.

Steneosaurus (STEN-ee-oh-SORE-us)

Age: Jurassic to Cretaceous

Size: 3–13 ft long

Weight: 200–300 lbs

Location: Estuaries and coastal waters near Europe, Africa

Food: Carnivore

Like modern turtles, Steneosaurus may have crawled onto land to lay its eggs. It had a long body, but had not developed fins. Its body was heavily armored as protection from attack by predators. Jaws lined with sharp teeth suggest a diet of fish.

Early Birds

Birds began evolving from dinosaurs during the Jurassic period. Feathered but flightless, they started developing strong flight muscles, feathered tails, and talons over millions of years. To save weight for flying, they also lost the need for teeth.

Shenshiornis primita

Confuciusornis (con-FEW-shus-OR-niss)

Age: Cretaceous, 130–120 mya
Size: 1 foot long
Weight: 1 lb
Location: China
Food: Herbivore

One of the earliest beaked and toothless bird species, which probably subsisted on a diet of seeds, it developed a short, feathered tail but still lacked powerful flight muscles. Confuciusornis was abundant species as indicated by thousands of fossil finds in China.

Hesperornis (hess-per-ORE-niss)

Age: Cretaceous, 75 mya
Size: 6 ft long
Weight: 10–20 lbs
Location: USA
Food: Carnivore

Hesperornis was a huge shorebird. If it had had the power of flight, it lost it to become an excellent diver. Big, wide feet helped propel it through the water as it chased fish and squid. It had wing-like arms that it used to steer through the water.

Iberomesornis (i-beh-row-may-SORE-us)

Age: Cretaceous, 135–120 mya
Size: 8 in long
Weight: 2 oz
Location: Spain
Food: Carnivore

About the size of a robin, Iberomesornis had the strong chest muscles and short tail need for flying. It also had curved talons for gripping tree branches. Its wings still had large claws on one finger, a holdover from its dinosaur roots.

Ichthyornis (ICK-thee-OR-niss)

Age: Cretaceous, 90–75 mya
Size: 2 ft long
Weight: 5 lbs
Location: USA
Food: Carnivore

The "fish bird" was about the size of a seagull except that its head and beak were larger, probably as a more effective means of catching and gripping fish. It had webbed feet and short claws, plus powerful breast muscles needed for flying.

DIGGING DEEPER

Extinction

By the end of the Cretaceous Period, dinosaurs were flourishing. They had become more diverse than ever before and were continuing to evolve. Herbivores developed protective armor to repel carnivores, which had become bigger, faster, and more powerful. Dinosaurs had been the dominant animal across the world for more than 186 million years, successfully adapting to changing climates, shifting land masses, and a violent world. Then, they were gone.

Scientists came up with all kinds of theories as to what destroyed these huge and amazing creatures so quickly and suddenly. Rapid and severe climate change, a deadly disease, a change in the Earth's orbit, radiation from a nearby supernova, and predators eating too many dinosaur eggs are some of the explanations put forward.

Two theories in combination seem to provide the best answer, and the one most paleontologists accept. The first is a meteorite strike, one large enough to create so much havoc that life could not go on. The other is volcanoes—lots of them—spewing debris and gases.

Geologists searching for oil in the 1970s made some peculiar findings that provided evidence of a large meteorite strike. About a mile underground, they found a layer of quartz that had been changed by immense pressure, the kind of pressure present during meteor strikes and nuclear blasts. They also found lumps of glass called tektites. These occur naturally from rocks exposed to both extreme heat and pressure, the kind produced by a large meteorite impact.

The most peculiar discovery was a distortion in the gravitational pull in one area. To understand that, you have to realize that everything has some gravitational pull—buildings, rocks, even you. The amount of mass an object has determines how much pull the object has. So, something as large as the Earth has enough pull to keep us and everything else from floating off into space. But a rock in your driveway does not have as much mass, so we cannot even feel its pull.

Something fractured the rock under the Mexican town Chicxulub, so much so that the density below town changed. It got lower. If you walk around Chicxulub, you weigh a little less than you do elsewhere in Mexico. Scientists realized they were drilling and working in a place where a massive meteorite had once struck the Earth. But an impact that large would have left behind a crater, and they could not find one. They realized an impact of this magnitude would have left behind an enormous crater, so they expanded their search area and started using special equipment that could detect changes in magnetism and gravity.

Then they found it. A crater 110 miles wide, partially submerged in waters off the west coast of Mexico. That crater was within a wide, 186-mile circle. The meteorite or asteroid producing that massive a crater was at least 6 miles wide and was traveling at an alarming 43,000 mph when it hit the Earth.

Checking sites around the world for further evidence, geologists probed a layer of clay that marked the end of the Cretaceous Period and the beginning of the next geological era—the same time the dinosaurs disappeared. They found extremely high amounts of a substance called iridium that is rare on Earth, but common in meteorites. That layer had iridium present in an amount 1,000 times higher than the neighboring layers above and below.

During the very late Cretaceous Period, volcanic eruptions in what is now western India began to increase. In 2015, scientists studying a 200,000 square mile rock formation in India called the Deccan Traps found evidence of an elevated number of volcanic eruptions around the same time the asteroid hit. The impact may have been strong enough to accelerate volcanic activity.

The result was a blanket of toxic gases, dust, and debris that covered the Earth. The dust cloud would have been thick enough to drop temperatures on the ground and block light from the sun. Plants and trees would have died, leaving no food for hungry herbivores that needed 400 pounds or more of vegetation daily. Carnivores that survived breathing dangerous gases would have had little to eat as the herbivores died. They could scavenge dead carcasses for a while but, eventually, maybe over several thousand more years, very little food was left. About 70% of all plant and animal life on land and in the waters perished.

The dinosaurs were gone. Along with them went the flying reptile pterosaurs and the mighty ocean-dwelling animals. Anything larger than a dog could not find enough food to survive. Those that did make it had already found new ways to live. Birds could fly to new areas in search of food. Scavengers surely had plenty of food available as other animals died. Small reptiles found even smaller organisms on which to feed. Jellyfish, turtles, sharks, and many other fish, crocodiles, lizards, scorpions, and insects all adapted to the new world.

So did mammals. Those tiny, scurrying rodent-like creatures surged in size and number. As the dust finally settled and the sun shone once again, plants returned. Mammals adapted to eating them without competition from dinosaurs. Over the next 20 million years or so, they increased in size so that many of their ancestors were 1,000 times larger. The Mesozoic Era ended as the Cenozoic Era began. It was time for the rise of the mammals.

Liopleurodon attacks Eurhinosaurus

Dinosaur Bites
Activities and More

The Mesozoic Era Timeline

TRIASSIC	JURASSIC	CRETACEOUS
250–201 MYA	201–145 MYA	145–65 MYA

Coelophysis

Plateosaurus

Pantydraco

Blikanasaurus

Herrerasaurus

Liliensternus

Anchisaurus

Archaeopteryx

Apatosaurus

Gargoyleosaurus

Anchiornis

Spinosaurus

Ankylosaurus

Chasmosaurus

Amargasaurus

Create Your Own Dinosaur

After reading all about the dinosaurs that once thrived on Earth, creating your own dinosaur may have crossed your mind. Or maybe you thought about what a brand new dinosaur species you discover might look like. Well, here's a chance to get creative and design your own dinosaur. These thoughts will get you started:

- Is your dinosaur an herbivore, carnivore, or omnivore?
- Does it stand on its hind legs, or on all fours?
- How tall is it?
- Is it feathered, armored, or scaly?
- What color is it?
- How is the head shaped?
- What do its teeth look like?
- How much does it weigh?
- Which time period did it live in?
- Is it tall and heavy, or shorter and fast moving?
- Where in the world did your dinosaur live?
- How long is its tail? Long for balance or shorter for maneuvering?
- Think about how you would describe your dinosaur to a paleontologist friend.
- What is your dinosaur's name? Did you also give it a species name?
- What dinosaurs preyed on your creation or find?
- If it's a carnivore, what did it eat—fish, reptiles, mammals, other dinosaurs—and which ones?
- If you have an herbivore, how much food did it need to survive?

Match the Tracks

1

2

3

Stegosaurus

Allosaurus

Deinonychus

Iguanodon

Tyrannosaurus

Triceratops

4

5

6

Answers on page 160.

Let's Go Fossil Hunting

You can discover fossils almost anywhere. Some of the best locations are along a stream, lake, or ocean, where the constant action of water uncovers the riches below the soil. A shovel, a brush, and a magnifying glass make a great fossil hunting kit. However, you may not need to dig or carry along any special tools to find fossils near water. You might also need a journal for keeping track of your finds, a camera for when you may not be able to keep the fossil, and a colander or other sifting device for removing dirt from around rocks.

Some public and private lands in the United States and throughout the world allow fossil hunting. If you live near one of these locations, or plan to vacation close to one, you might want to set aside some time for a fossil hunt:

1. **Big Brook—New Jersey:** About an hour's drive from New York City. Finds date back to the late Cretaceous Period and include a variety of teeth from sharks and swimming reptiles.

2. **Dinosaur Valley State Park—Texas:** Find dinosaur footprints embedded along the creek bed. Explore the stream banks for tooth and bone fragments.

3. **Fossil Park—Ohio:** A quarry that dates back to the Devonian Period, which occurred before the arrival of the dinosaurs. This site is completely free of charge.

4. **Hell Creek Beds—Montana:** This area of rock formations dates back to the late Cretaceous Period. You can explore the area on a guided tour with a paleontologist. Hadrosaurs and theropods once roamed the region, and their fossils can still be found there.

5. **Montour Preserve—Pennsylvania:** Around 230 miles northeast of Pittsburgh, the site dates to the Devonian Period. Dig for fossils and keep what you find.

6. **Purse State Park—Maryland:** Shark teeth and shells from the Paleocene Period are among the fossilized finds here.

7. **Red Gulch Dinosaur Tracksite—Wyoming:** The staff can help identify dinosaur tracks. You can fossil hunt and keep any small shells and trilobites you find without a permit. However, deeper exploration for teeth, bones, and vertebrates requires a permit. This site dates back around 167 mya.

8. **Westmoreland State Park—Virginia:** Find fossilized teeth from ancient sharks and swimming reptiles. Some tooth finds have been as large as an adult's hand.

Test Your Dino Know-How

1. What period had the greatest diversity of dinosaur species?
   a. Triassic   b. Jurassic   c. Cretaceous   d. Diatomic

2. Which is not a dinosaur?
   a. Dakosaurus
   b. Spinophorosaurus
   c. Troodon
   d. Bambiraptor

3. Who or what was Leonardo?
   a. The nickname given to a well-preserved dinosaur
   b. The creator of the Da Vinci code
   c. A famous fossil hunter
   d. A 19th-century novelist

4. Which is considered to have been the smartest dinosaur?
   a. Brontosaurus
   b. Tyrannosaurus
   c. Troodon
   d. Stegosaurus

5. Which most likely led to the mass extinction that occurred at the end of the Cretaceous Period?
   a. A disease that spread through dinosaur colonies
   b. Major volcanic eruptions along with a meteorite strike
   c. Overhunting by predators
   d. It was just their time

6. All of the following are ways scientists determine the age of a fossil except:
   a. Age of the fossil compared to surrounding rock
   b. Radioactive decay
   c. The direction magnetic rocks point
   d. Sunspot activity

7. Why is Cryolophosaurus nicknamed Elvisaurus?
   a. Elvis made the first discovery
   b. Its head crest looked like a hairstyle worn by a famous singer
   c. The first of its species was found near Memphis, TN
   d. It could make song-like vocalizations

8. Which was the largest dinosaur?
   a. Diplodocus
   b. Apatosaurus
   c. Brachiosaurus
   d. Argentinosaurus

Answers on page 160.

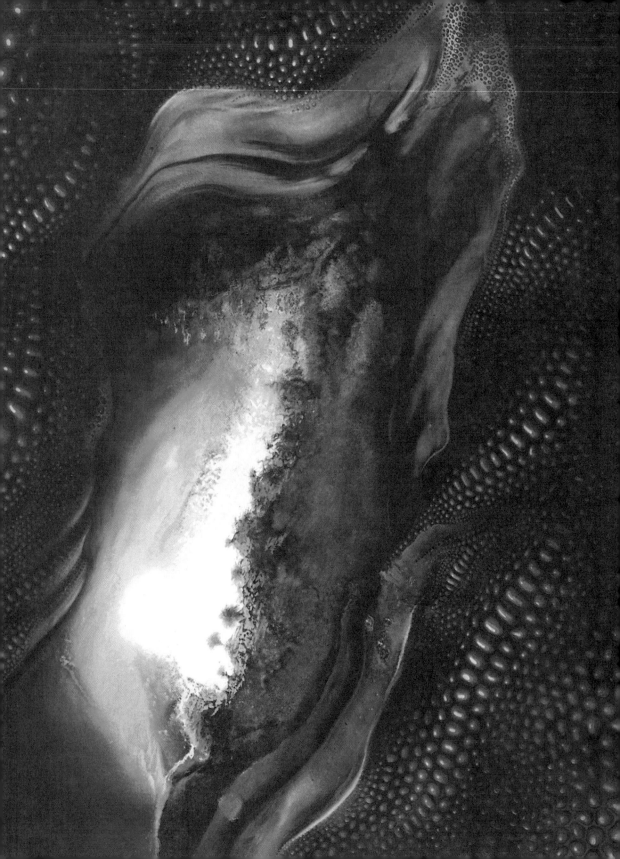

Bibliography

Books

Barnes-Svarney, P., & Svarney, T. E. (2010). *The handy dinosaur answer book* (2nd ed.). Canton, MI: Visible Ink Press.

DK Publishing. (2007). *First dinosaur encyclopedia*. New York, NY: Author.

DK Publishing. (2011). *Dinosaurs: A visual encyclopedia*. New York, NY: Author.

Lambert, D. (1993). *The ultimate dinosaur book*. New York, NY: DK Publishing.

Parker, S. (2003). *1000 things you should know about dinosaurs*. Essex, England: Miles Kelly Publishing.

Pim, K., & Horner, J. (2014). *Dinosaurs: The grand tour: Everything worth knowing about dinosaurs from Aaardonyx to Zuniceratops*. New York, NY: The Experiment.

Websites

DinoDictionary.com. (n.d.). *Dinosaurs from A–Z*. Retrieved from http://www.dinodictionary.com

Enchanted Learning. (n.d.). *Zoom dinosaurs*. Retrieved from http://www.enchantedlearning.com/subjects/dinosaurs

EnvironmentalScience.org. (n.d.). *What is a paleontologist?*. Retrieved from http://www.environmentalscience.org/career/paleontologist

Mikkelson, D. (2015). *Eggs-Terminated*. Retrieved from http://www.snopes.com/politics/satire/dinosaur.asp

Paleontological Research Institution. (n.d.). *I want to be a paleontologist*. Retrieved from https://www.priweb.org/outreach.php?page=Edu_Prog/publicEdprograms/be_a_paleontologist

Prehistoric-Wildlife.com. (n.d.). Retrieved from http://www.prehistoric-wildlife.com

Switek, B. (2009). So you want to be a paleontologist?. *Smithsonian Magazine*. Retrieved from http://www.smithsonianmag.com/science-nature/so-you-want-to-be-a-paleontologist-43495392/?no-ist

Watry, G. (2015). Chemical analysis finds pigments persist in dino feathers. *R&D Magazine*. Retrieved from http://www.rdmag.com/articles/2015/09/chemical-analysis-finds-pigments-persist-dino-feathers

Epidexipteryx and Nephila

About the Author

Bob Korpella is a freelance writer and nature photographer. He has earned certification as a Master Naturalist, serving as program chair, vice president, and president of the Springfield, MO, chapter over the past several years. As a naturalist, Bob presents programs to students from preschool to high school on topics as diverse as stream ecology, fur bearers, insects, bats, and owls. He also participates in bird surveys and monitors the health of streams at 14 different sites in southwest Missouri. He has received a Choose Environmental Excellence, Water Warrior, and Stream Team Ambassador Award.

Bob's nature photography has been featured in the Missouri Department of Conservation nature calendar and wildlife magazines. As a writer, Bob's work has appeared in newspapers across the country as well as *National Geographic*'s Green Living.

Bob calls the Ozarks region of Missouri and Arkansas home. He is a graduate of the University of Arkansas. He and his wife live in Mountain Home, where they enjoy frequent visits from their two daughters and their grandchildren. Bob also loves to camp, hike, kayak, fish, and hunt.

Index of Species

Image Credits

The publisher would like to thank the following for their permission to reproduce their illustrations:

Abbreviation key: t–top; m–middle; b–bottom

12: Sergey Krasovskiy (t/m), James Kuether (b); 13: Emilio Rolandi (t), Corey Ford (b); 14: Jeffrey Martz (t); 15: Nobumichi Tamura (t), James Kuether (b); 16: Commander-Salamander (b); 17: James Kuether (t); 18: Sergey Krasovskiy (t), Nobumichi Tamura (m), Goran Bogicevic (b); 21: Cisiopurple (t), Russell Gooday (m); 26: Eduardo Camargo (t); 28: James Kuether (t), Discover Magazine (b); 29: Sergey Krasovskiy (t), 30: James Kuether (b); 31: Peter Montgomery (b); 35: Sergey Krasovskiy (t/b); 36: James Kuether (t); 37: Sergey Krasovskiy (t); 38: Sergey Krasovskiy (t); 39: Cheung Chung Tat (b); 41: James Kuether (t), Sergey Krasovskiy (b); 42: Audrey Atuchin (b); 43: Sergey Krasovskiy (t); 44: Sergey Krasovskiy (t), Masato Hattori (b); 45: Sergey Krasovskiy (b); 46: James Kuether (t/b); 47: Nobumichi Tamura (t); 48: Sergey Krasovskiy (t); 49: Cisiopurple (b); 51: Sergey Krasovskiy (b); 52: Cheung Chung Tat (t), James Kuether (b); 53: Sergey Krasovskiy (b); 56: Sergey Krasovskiy (t/b); 58: Peter Montgomery (t); 59: Sergey Krasovskiy (b); 60: Sergey Krasovskiy (t/b); 61: Brian Choo (t); 62: H. Kyoht Luterman (t), Cisiopurple (b); 63: H. Kyoht Luterman (t), Camus Altamirano (b); 64: James Kuether (t); 65: Sergey Krasovskiy (t/b); 68: James Kuether (t), Sergey Krasovskiy (b); 69: Sergey Krasovskiy (t); 70: Sergey Krasovskiy (b); 71: Sergey Krasovskiy (t/b); 72: Nobumichi Tamura (t/b); 73: Ezequiel Vera (b); 74: Sergey Krasovskiy (t); 78: Sergey Krasovskiy (t); 79: Sergey Krasovskiy (b); 80: Eduardo Camargo (b); 81: H. Kyoht Luterman (t), Sergey Krasovskiy (b); 82: Sergey Krasovskiy (t); 84: Lida Xing and Yi Liu (b); 86: Sergey Krasovskiy (t); 89: Diego Barletta (b); 91: Sergey Krasovskiy (t); 93: Sergey Krasovskiy (t); 94: James Kuether (b); 95: Sergey Krasovskiy (t); 96: Sergey Krasovskiy (b); 97: Fred Wierum (t); 98: James Kuether (t); 99: Nicholas Nordby (t); 100: Sergey Krasovskiy (t); 101: Sergey Krasovskiy (t/b); 102: Sergey Krasovskiy (t); 103: Julius Csotonyi (t); 105: Sergey Krasovskiy (t); 108: Masato Hattori (b); 109: Emily Willoughby (t), James Kuether (b); 115: Sergey Krasovskiy (b); 116: James Kuether (b); 117: Connie Ma (b); 118: Raul Martin (b); 123: Joschua Knüppe (t); 124: Sergey Krasovskiy (t); 125: American Museum of Natural History (t); 131: Alexey Katz (t), Jeffrey Martz (m); 138: Nobumichi Tamura (b); 139: James Kuether (t); 141: Sergey Krasovskiy (b); 142: Sergey Krasovskiy (b); 143: James Kuether (m); 144: Sergey Krasovskiy (b); 145: Masato Hattori (t); 146: Eduardo Camargo (t), Nobumichi Tamura (b); 147: Allison Elaine Johnson (m); 148: Sergio Pérez (t), Antonella Galizia (b); 149: Feliks; 153: Sergey Krasovskiy, James Kuether; 160: Sergey Krasovskiy; 165: Sergey Krasovskiy.

What Is a Paleoartist?

How do you breathe life into creatures that perished millions of years ago? Ask a paleoartist! Without a complete specimen to examine, these folks take written descriptions of dinosaurs, the images of dinosaur bones or skeletons, a knowledge of muscles and skin, and create an illustration of what each dinosaur species must have looked like. The illustrations in this book are the work of some very talented paleoartists.

Proceratosaurus

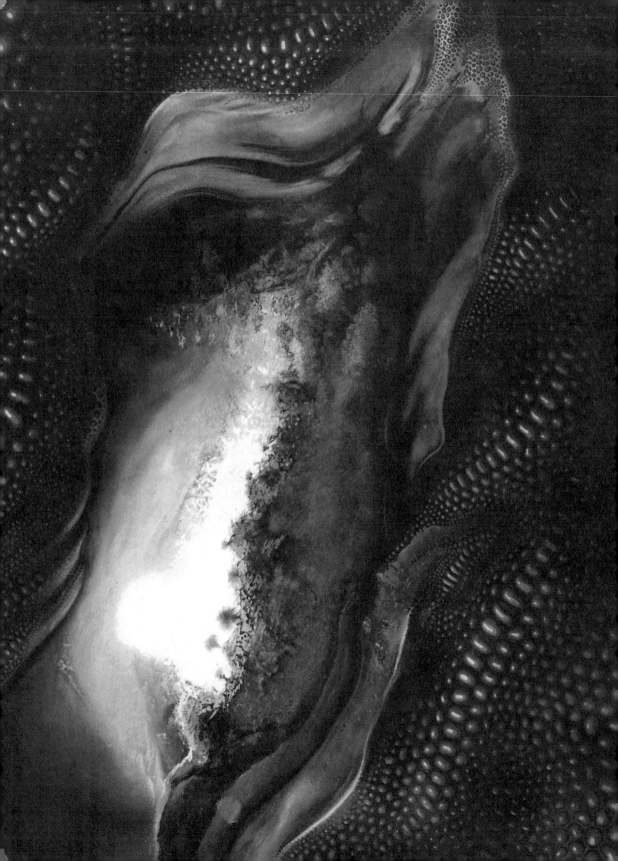